Mastery of Music Theory

a text and workbook

Book 2: Diatonic Harmonization
Second Edition

Brian Kehlenbach

Mastery of Music Theory, Book 2:
Diatonic Harmonization

A Text and Workbook

Second Edition

EBK Music

Copyright © 2023, 2014 by Brian Kehlenbach

Contents

Chapter 1: Diatonic Chords within the Major Key 1
The Diatonic Triads 1

Chapter 2: Piano Voicing with Primary Triads 7
Primary Triads 7
Harmonizing a Simple Melody 7
Piano Voicing 8

Chapter 3: Diatonic Chords within the Minor Key 13
Diatonic Chords Using the Harmonic Minor Scale 13
Diatonic Triads from the Melodic Minor Scale 14

Chapter 4: Four-Part Chorale Style Writing 19
The Standard Voice Ranges 19
Voicing In Four Parts with Close Spacing 19
Voicing In Four Parts with Open Spacing 21

Chapter 5: Voice Leading and Forbidden Parallels 27
The Four Types of Motion 27
General Characteristics of Four-Part Chorale Style Voice Leading 28
Forbidden Parallels 29
Direct 5ths and 8ves 33

Chapter 6: Progression and Voice Leading with I, IV, V 35
Harmonic Function 35
Authentic, Plagal, and Half Cadences 35
Perfect and Imperfect Cadences 37
Root Tone Motion 38
Voice Leading Procedures for Root Tone Motion in 5ths 39
Voice Leading for Root Tone Motion in 2nds 41
Forbidden Melodic Intervals 42

Chapter 7: Harmonizing Melody: More Considerations 51
Choosing Harmonies 51
Alternative Voice Leading Methods for Root Tone Motion in 5ths 53

Chapter 8: Secondary Triads 57
Tonal Functions of Primary and Secondary Triads 57
Root Tone Motion in Thirds 58
The Deceptive Cadence 59

Chapter 9: First Inversion Triads 67
First Inversion Triads 67
Doubling of First Inversion Major and Minor Triads 67
Labeling of First Inversion Triads 67
Usages of First Inversion Triads 68
Overlapped Voices 68
Examples of Doubling in First Inversion Major and Minor Triads 69
Diminished Triads in First Inversion: Usage and Doubling 70
The Phrygian Half Cadence 71

Chapter 10: Second Inversion Triads: The Cadential $^6_4$ 77
Second Inversion Triads 77
The Arpeggiating $^6_4$ Chord 77
The Cadential $^6_4$ Chord 78
Rhythmic Placement of the Cadential $^6_4$ Chord 78

Chapter 11: The Pedal and Passing $^6_4$ 83
The Passing $^6_4$ Chord 83
The Pedal $^6_4$ Chord 84

Chapter 12: The Dominant 7th 91
Seventh Chords 91
Voice Leading with the Dominant 7 Chord 91
Downward Resolution of the Leading Tone in an Inner Voice 93

Chapter 13: Inversions of Dominant 7th 101
Inversions of the Seventh Chord 101

Chapter 14: Other Diatonic Seventh Chords 105
Qualities of Seventh Chords 105
The ii7 and iiø7 Chords 106
The viiø7 and viio7 Chords 107

Chapter 15: Seventh Chord Sequence in 5ths 113
The Authentic Harmonic Sequence 113

Appendix A: Keys Around the Circle of Fifths 117

Appendix B: Qualities of Triads and Seventh Chords 119

Appendix C: Non Chord Tones 1 121
    Passing Tone (PT) 121
    Neighbor Tone (NT) 121
    Anticipation (ant.) 122
    Escape Tone (E.T.) 122
    Appoggiatura (app.) 122
    Neighbor Group (Changing Tones) (N.G.) 123
    Incomplete Neighbor Tone (I.N.T) 123
    Pedal Point (Pedal Tone) (Ped.) 124
    Application of Non-Chord Tones 125

Appendix D: Non Chord Tones 2, The Suspension 127

Appendix E: Figured Bass Harmonization 133

Appendix F: Piano Harmonization Exercises 135

Appendix G: Repertoire for Analysis 139

Appendix H: Harmonization Project 159

Appendix I: Check Your Understanding Answers 161

Chapter 1: Diatonic Chords within the Major Key

Terms and Concepts in This Chapter		
scale degrees	mediant	leading tone
diatonic triads	submediant	Roman numerals
tonic	dominant	pop chord symbols
supertonic	submediant	upper and lower case Roman numerals

The Diatonic Triads

For each key, there is a set of triads that can be built above each pitch within the scale. These scale pitches are called **scale degrees**. To construct these triads, first build a major scale, and then build the triads in third intervals above each scale degree using notes that fit in the key signature. Such a system that is based only on the notes of a particular major or minor scale is called **diatonic**.

Below is a chart of the diatonic triads that fit in the key of C major. Notice that the scale degrees are written underneath using the convention $\hat{1}$, $\hat{2}$, $\hat{3}$, etc. This is the standard way to designate scale degrees.

Example 1.1 - The Diatonic Triads In C Major with Scale Degrees

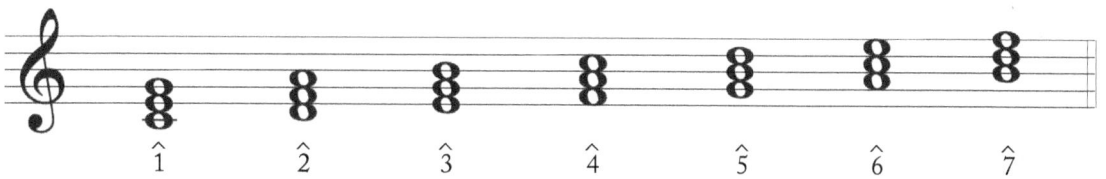

The scale degrees and corresponding chords can also be named using the following traditional terminology:

Example 1.2 - Descriptive Names for the Scale Degrees

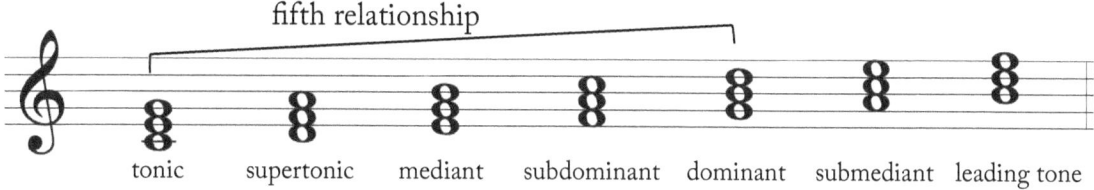

The term **tonic** refers to the first note of the diatonic scale and its associated chord. Music tends to begin with and ultimately return to the tonic. **Supertonic** is, quite simply, the note (and associated chord) a step above the tonic. **Dominant** implies a fifth relationship, and as you can see from the diagram above, it is located a fifth above tonic. The **mediant** occupies an intermediary position between the tonic and the dominant. The other terms are easier to explain if we show a chart that includes a tonic chord at the top of the scale:

Example 1.3 - The Subdominant and Submediant

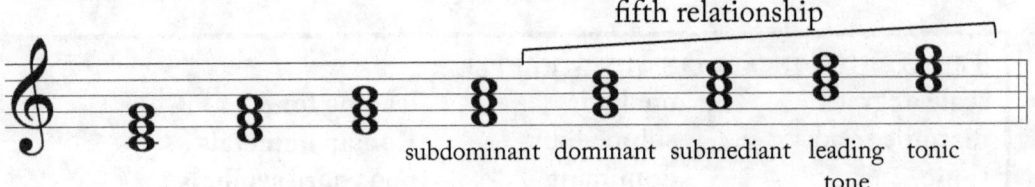

Example 1.3 illustrates that the **subdominant** is a fifth <u>lower</u> than the tonic chord found at the top of the scale. It is named subdominant because of this relationship and not because it is a step lower than the dominant. Consequently, the **submediant** refers to a scale degree that is directly between the subdominant and the tonic, as shown in example 1.3.

The **leading tone** is the last note of the ascending scale before returning to the tonic, and it sounds as though it is "leading" back to the tonic. If you play these chords on the piano, you will hear the sound of the leading tone chord resolving up to the tonic chord.

The chords within the key can be analyzed as either major, minor, or diminished triads. Below is another chart of the triads, this time using **Roman numeral** labels as well as **pop chord symbol** labels to designate the chord qualities. Keep in mind that the quality of the triads as they relate to the scale degree will always be the same in all major keys: the I, IV and V chords are always major; the ii, iii, and vi chords are always minor; and the vii° chord is alwaays diminished in every major key.

Example 1.4 - Pop Chord Symbols and Roman Numerals

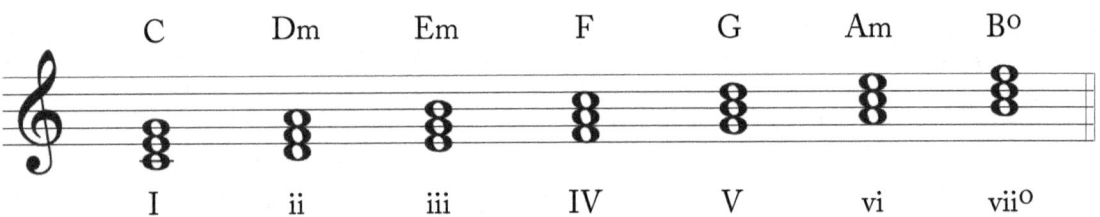

While the Roman numeral labels are quite similar to the scale degree labels used in example 1.1, they also offer an advantage in that we can use **upper case Roman numerals** to designate major triads and **lower case Roman numerals** to designate minor triads. The small circle (°) on the vii° chord indicates that its quality is diminished. We indicate the diminished quality with both the small circle and the lower case Roman numeral (vii°).

Check Your Understanding 1.1

For each example, write the triad pitches for the scale degree in the indicated major key. Write the appropriate Roman numeral and pop chord symbol beneath each.

1. key: C $\hat{4}$
2. key: G $\hat{7}$
3. key: E♭ $\hat{5}$
4. key: B $\hat{2}$

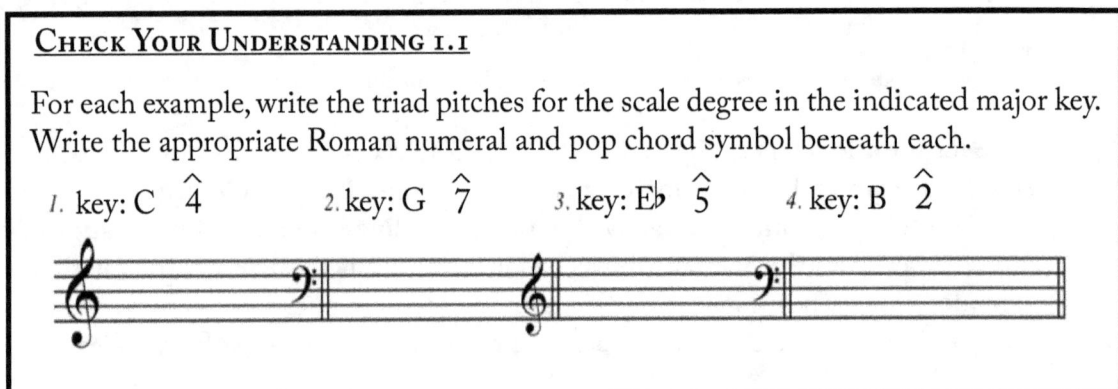

Exercise 1.1

For each example, the first note of a major scale is given. Write the key signature of the note that you see, and then draw in each note of the scale. Add in the notes of the triads above each scale degree. Place the proper pop chord symbols above and the Roman numeral designation below each chord. The first two examples have been done for you. Notice that the notes that are affected by the key signature have been colored in. You should do this in your answers as well.

4

pop chord symbols:

7

Roman numerals:

pop chord symbols:

8

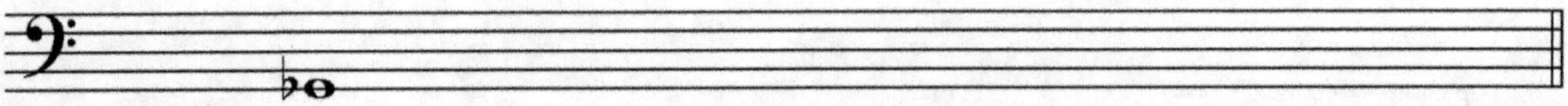

Roman numerals:

pop chord symbols:

9

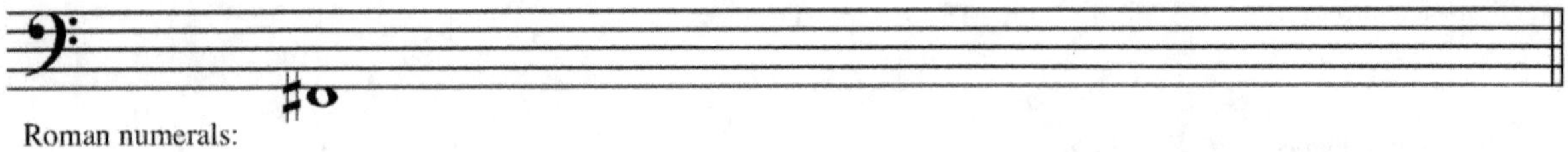

Roman numerals:

pop chord symbols:

10

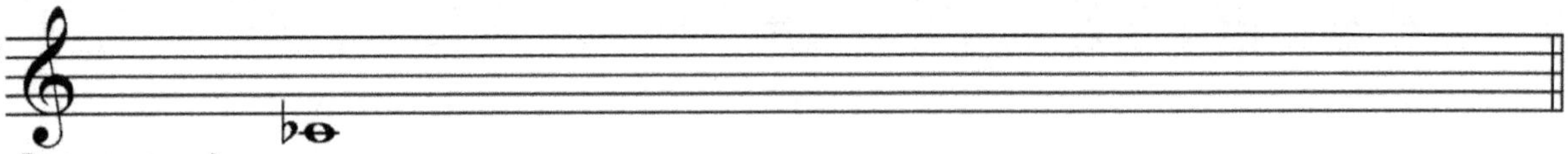

Roman numerals:

pop chord symbols:

11

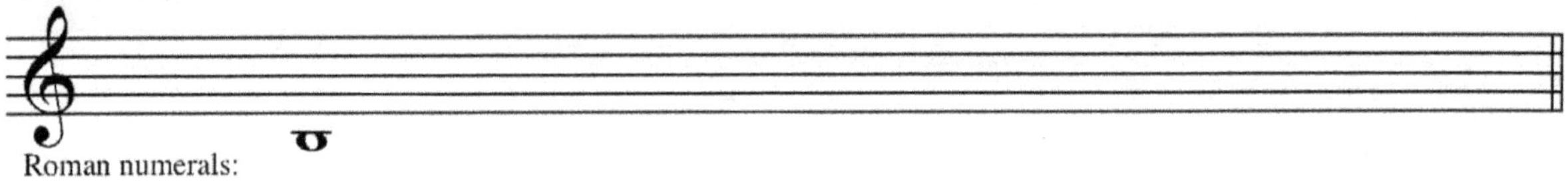

Roman numerals:

pop chord symbols:

12

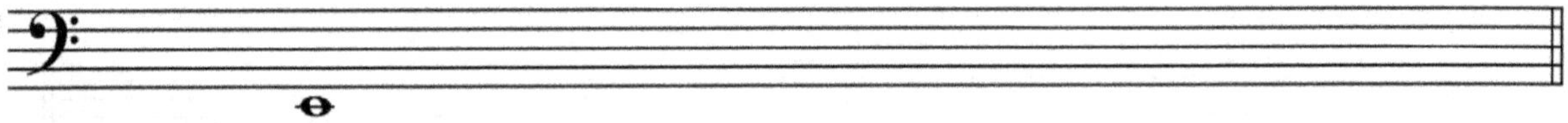

Roman numerals:

pop chord symbols:

13

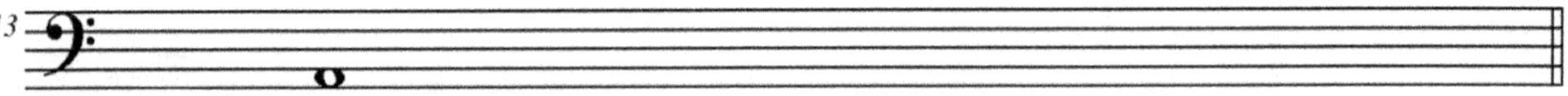

Roman numerals:

pop chord symbols:

14

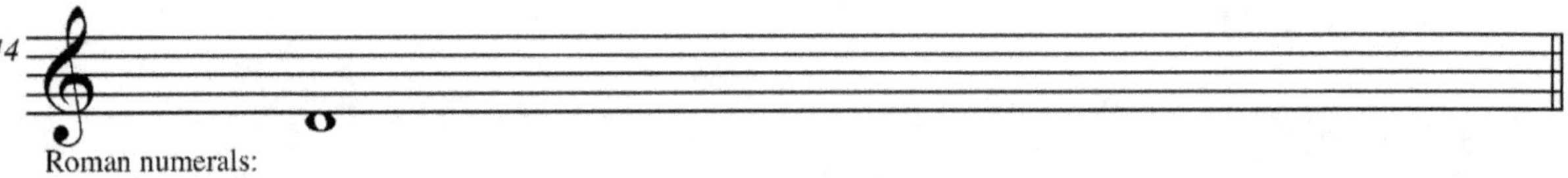

Roman numerals:

pop chord symbols:

15

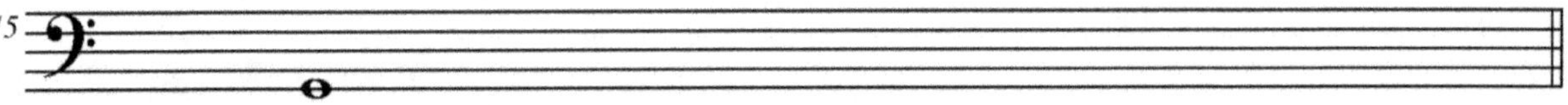

Roman numerals:

EXERCISE 1.2

For each example, first write the key signature. Then write the triad pitches for the indicated scale degree. Also, provide pop chord symbols and Roman numerals. The first example is done for you.

1. Key: B♭ $\hat{5}$
2. Key: A $\hat{2}$
3. Key: A♭ $\hat{6}$
4. Key: B $\hat{1}$

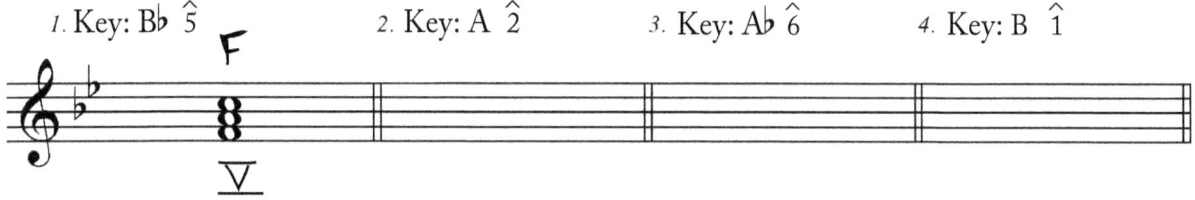

5. Key: G♭ $\hat{3}$
6. Key: E $\hat{4}$
7. Key: E♭ $\hat{7}$
8. Key F♯ $\hat{7}$

9. Key: D $\hat{5}$
10. Key: A♭ $\hat{2}$
11. Key: E $\hat{6}$
12. Key: C♯ $\hat{1}$

EXERCISE 1.3

For the next set of examples, follow the same procedure, but do not provide the key signature. Instead, provide all necessary accidentals with the triad. The first example is done for you.

13. Key: D $\hat{3}$
14. Key: D♭ $\hat{4}$
15. Key: A $\hat{7}$
16. Key: F $\hat{7}$

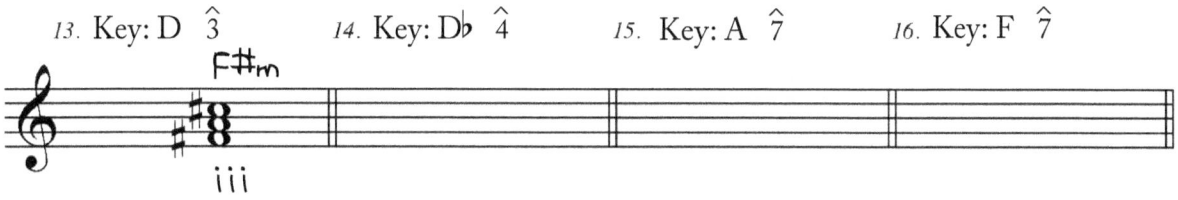

17. Key: C♭ $\hat{1}$
18. Key: G $\hat{2}$
19. Key: C $\hat{3}$
20. Key: B♭ $\hat{4}$

21. Key: E♭ $\hat{5}$
22. Key: B $\hat{6}$
23. Key: F♯ $\hat{5}$
24. Key: G♭ $\hat{6}$

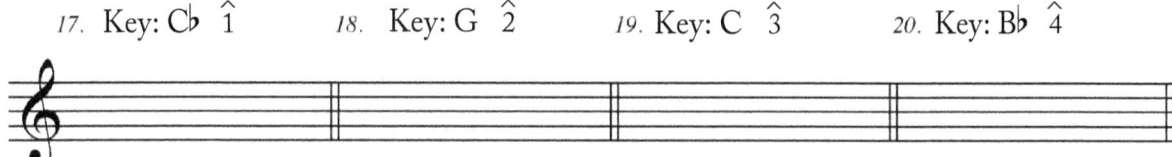

Chapter 2: Piano Voicing with Primary Triads

> TERMS AND CONCEPTS IN THIS CHAPTER
> **primary triads**   **piano voicing**   **close spacing**
> **harmonize**   **root position**

PRIMARY TRIADS

The tonic triad, together with those triads that have a fifth relationship with tonic, are called **primary triads**. These are the I (tonic), IV (subdominant), and V (dominant) chords. Remember that the dominant chord is found a fifth above tonic, and the subdominant chord is found a fifth below tonic.

EXAMPLE 2.1 - THE PRIMARY TRIADS

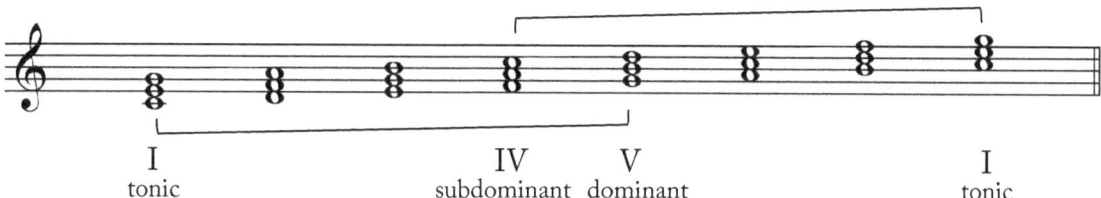

Using only these three primary chords, we can **harmonize** any note of the major scale. To harmonize means to add chord tones to a melody. To determine the available chords for harmonization, we simply find triads that include scale degrees that match with the melody notes. Some notes of the major scale can be harmonized by more than one primary chord, as shown in the chart below:

EXAMPLE 2.2 - THE PRIMARY TRIADS MATCHED WITH SCALE DEGREES

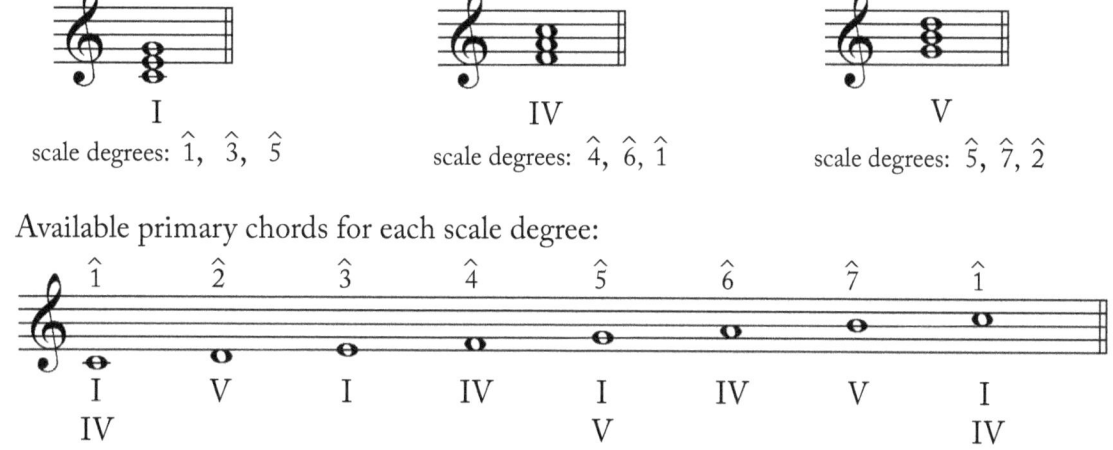

HARMONIZING A SIMPLE MELODY

Now, we should try to harmonize the following melody in the key of C major:

Example 2.3 - A Simple melody in C Major

To complete the harmonization, we first identify the primary chords to harmonize with the melodic pitches and then write in the Roman numerals underneath. We will continue to restrict ourselves to the primary chords (I, IV, and V) for the time being.

Example 2.4 - A Harmonization with Primary Triads

I   IV   I   V   I

Piano Voicing

Next, we will place the proper chord tones beneath the melodic tones. For this example, we will use a type of chord arrangement called **piano voicing**. Piano voicing involves placing three pitches in the treble clef to be played by the right hand and one pitch in the bass clef to be played by the left hand. To complete the right hand part, add below the melody note the two remaining pitches that will complete the harmony. Example 2.5 shows the first melodic pitch with harmony notes.

Example 2.5

Since we need to harmonize the first melody note, E, with a I chord, we add in the remaining pitches C and G. These pitches are placed below the melody pitch, but as close as possible to the melody pitch.

Next we should add in the bass note to be played by the left hand. For this, we will write the root tone of the chord. Whenever the root tone is in the lowest (bass) position, the chord is in **root position**.

Example 2.6

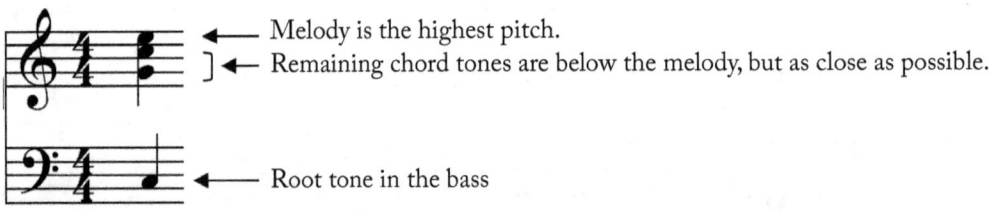

— Melody is the highest pitch.
— Remaining chord tones are below the melody, but as close as possible.

— Root tone in the bass

Observe the three notes in the treble clef. Notice that the distance between the upper note (the melody note E) and the lowest note (G) is less than an octave. For this reason, we can say that this chord is in **close spacing**. Close spacing is an arrangement of four notes in which the span of the upper three is less than an octave.

Now, we should complete the harmonization of our melody by continuing with piano voicing in close spacing.

EXAMPLE 2.7 - COMPLETED HARMONIZATION

You should play this example on the piano. You will notice that it is both sonorous and easy to play.

CHECK YOUR UNDERSTANDING 2.1
Complete these two short examples using piano voicing.

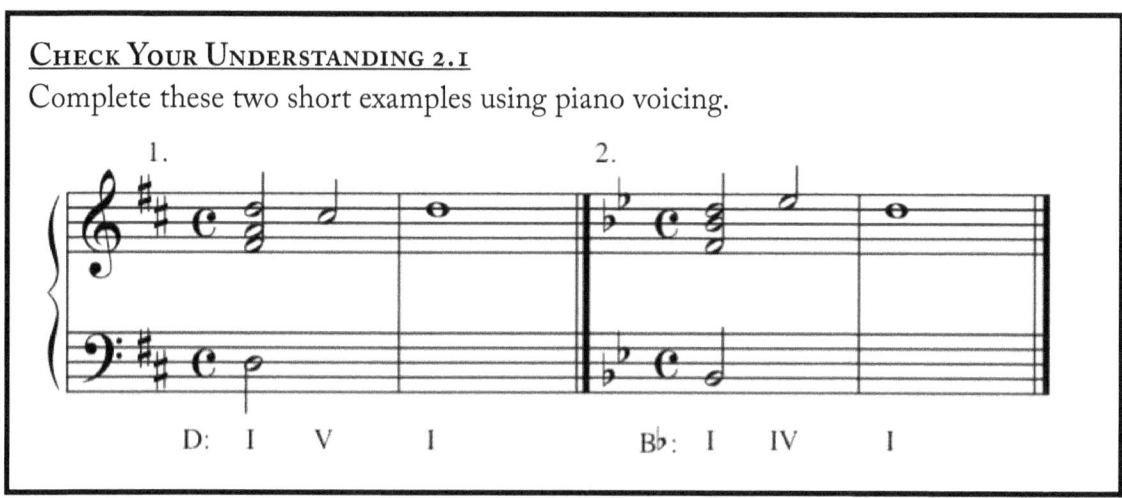

Exercise 2.1

Complete these harmonizations using piano voicing in close spacing. Make sure to identify the key for each example. The first example is done for you. The notes that are given should remain as the uppermost pitch of the voicing.

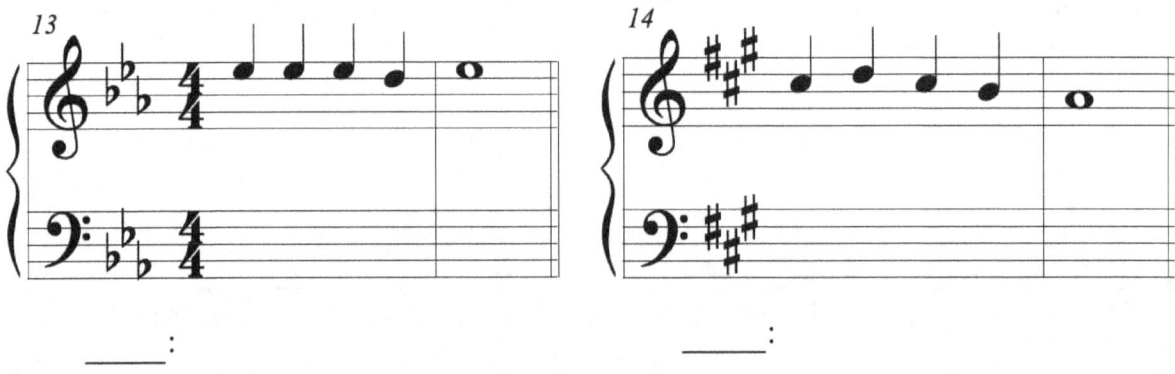

For these last two examples, fill in the Roman numerals and then complete the harmonizations.

Chapter 3: Diatonic Chords within the Minor Key

> **TERMS AND CONCEPTS IN THIS CHAPTER**
> **harmonic minor**   **melodic minor**
> **raised leading tone**

DIATONIC CHORDS USING THE HARMONIC MINOR SCALE

Just as we constructed a set of diatonic chords for the major key, we can also construct a set for the minor key. The situation is a bit more complicated in minor because of the three different forms of the minor scale: natural, harmonic, and melodic. The most useful scale for constructing harmonies is the **harmonic minor,** as implied by its name:

EXAMPLE 3.1 - THE C HARMONIC MINOR SCALE

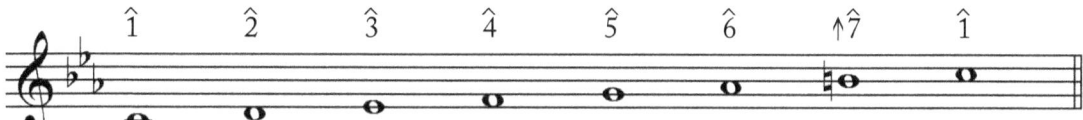

The harmonic minor scale has a **raised leading tone**. This scale alteration lends extra power for some harmonic progressions by creating a half step motion from the 7th degree ($\hat{7}$) back to tonic ($\hat{1}$). We will use this alteration when constructing triads that tend to progress back to the tonic chord, such as the V chord and the vii° chord. The V chord progresses back to the tonic because of its strong 5th relationship, and the vii° chord progresses back to tonic due to its close half-step proximity. In the chart below, the chord tone 3rd of the V chord and the root tone of the vii° chord have been raised to B♮. Note that the III chord in the chart below does not contain the alteration of B♮ because it does not normally progress back to the tonic.

EXAMPLE 3.2 - DIATONIC TRIADS IN THE C HARMONIC MINOR SCALE

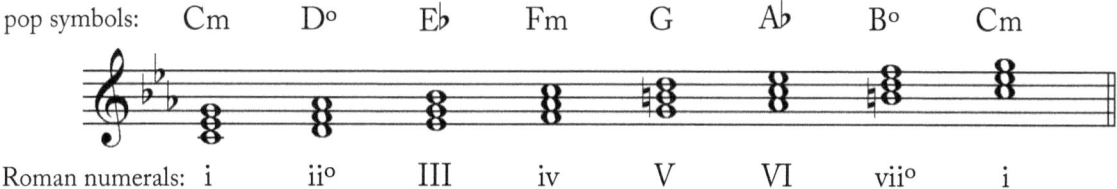

The primary chords in minor are the i, iv, and V, just as in major but with some different chord qualities. You should take note of the interesting variety of chord qualities available in the minor key. While it is possible to expand this set by considering other forms of the minor scale, the triads qualities in example 3.2 comprise the most common and standard set.

Another way to organize the chords is by their quality. In the chart below, each chord quality is associated with its Roman numeral positions in both the major and minor scales.

Example 3.3 - Comparison of Triad Qualities in Major and Minor Keys

	Major Key	Minor Key
Major Triads	I, IV, V	III, V, VI
Minor Triads	ii, iii, vi	i, iv
Diminished Triads	vii°	ii°, vii°

Notice from this chart that both the major and minor keys have a major triad on the 5th scale degree and a diminished triad on the 7th scale degree.

> ### Check Your Understanding 3.1
> For each example, write the triad pitches for the scale degree in the indicated minor key. Write the appropriate Roman numeral beneath each.
>
> 1. key: c $\hat{4}$
> 2. key: f $\hat{7}$
> 3. key: g $\hat{5}$
> 4. key: f♯ $\hat{2}$

Diatonic Triads from the Melodic Minor Scale

As you know, there are three versions of minor scales: natural minor, harmonic minor, and melodic minor. For this reason, the number of triads that are possible in a minor key is sometimes expanded from the standard harmonic minor set we have already determined. Most of these additional triads come about as a result of a melodic pattern in one of the voices that is following either the ascending or descending **melodic minor scale**. In the chart below, all the possible triads in melodic minor are shown. The triads that differ from our standard harmonic minor set are indicated with an asterisk (*). While these triad qualities are not as common, you will encounter them in musical literature, and they are provided here for your reference.

Example 3.4 - Chart of Diatonic Triads in C Melodic Minor

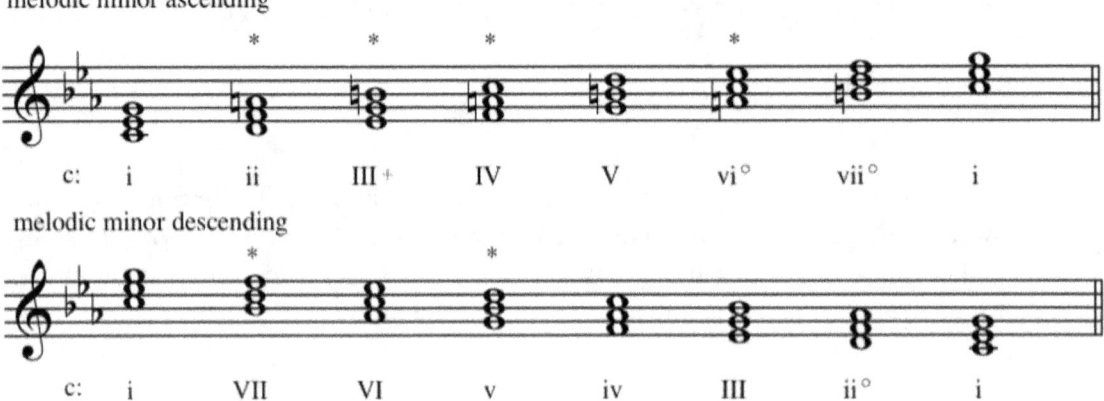

Exercise 3.1

For each example, write the minor key signature of the note that you see and then draw in each note of the harmonic minor scale. Add in the notes of the triad above each scale degree to build a standard set of triads in minor. Make sure to raise the leading tone ($\hat{7}$) in the V chord (the chord 3rd) and in the vii° chord (the root tone). Place the proper pop chord symbols above and the Roman numeral designation below each chord. The first two examples have been done for you.

Exercise 3.2

For each example, first write the minor key signature. Then write the triad pitches for the indicated scale degree. Also, name the chord with a pop chord symbol and Roman numeral. Make sure to raise the leading tone in all V and vii° chords. The first example is done for you.

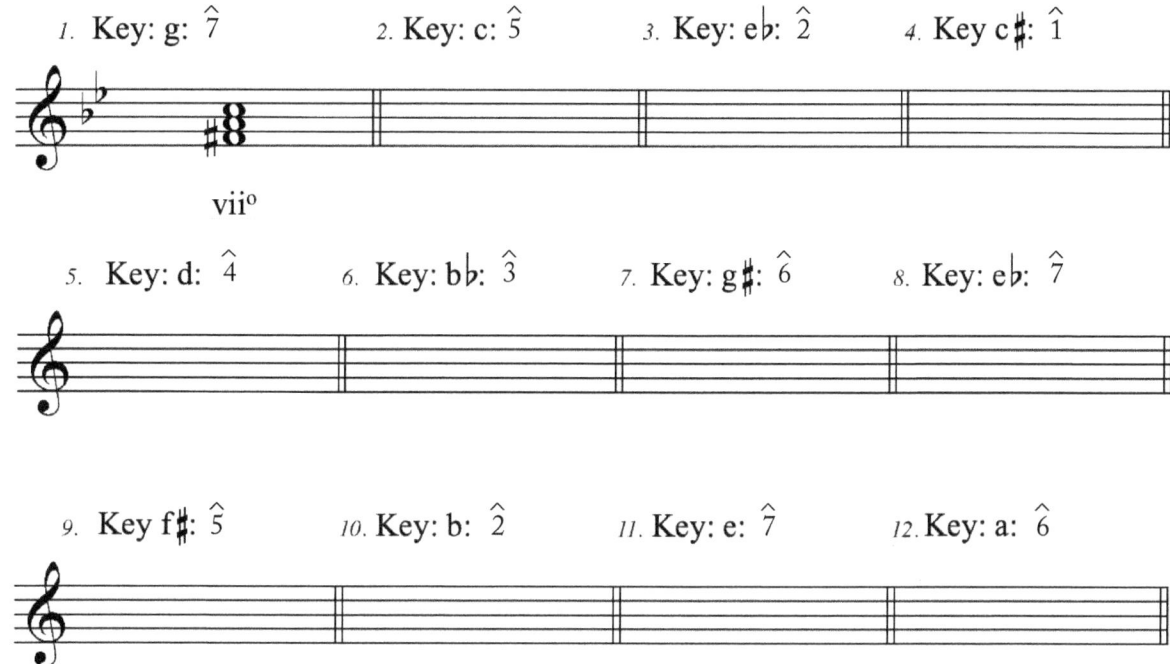

For the next set of examples, follow the same procedure, but do not provide the key signature. Instead, provide all necessary accidentals with the triad. The first example is done for you.

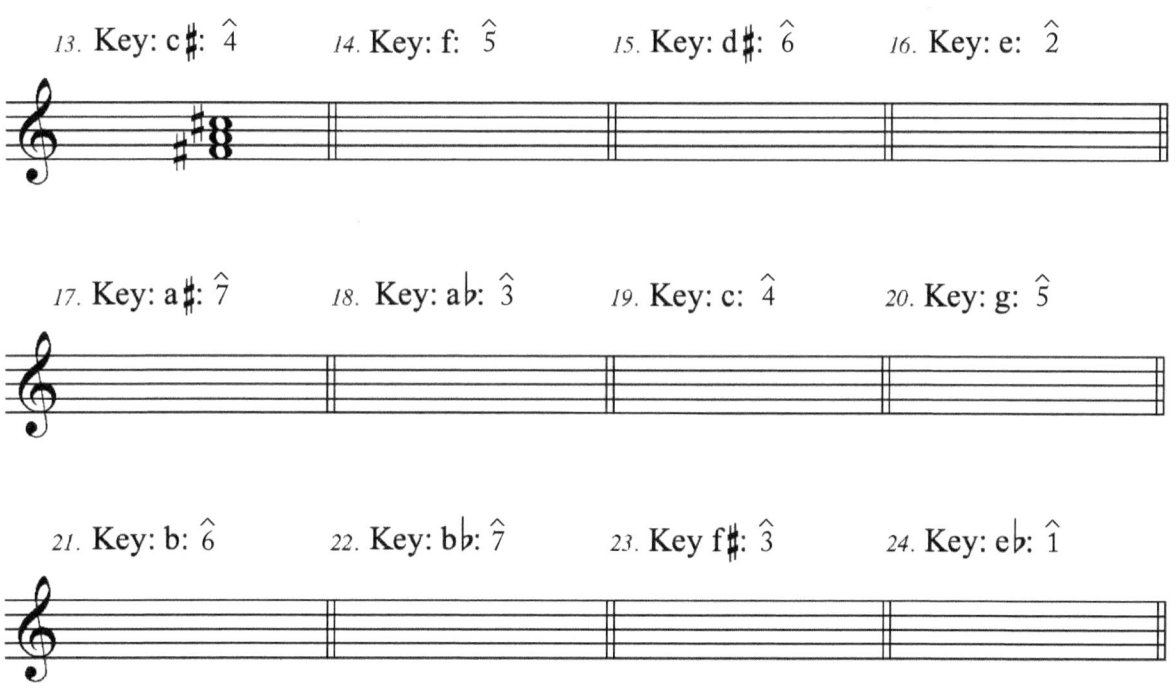

Chapter 4: Four-Part Chorale Style Writing

> **TERMS AND CONCEPTS IN THIS CHAPTER**
> soprano   bass   open spacing
> alto   close spacing   doubled pitch
> tenor

THE STANDARD VOICE RANGES

In four-part chorale style voicing, we harmonize using four voices: the **soprano**, **alto**, **tenor**, and **bass**. The normal ranges of these voices are given in the chart below, as special care must be given to write only pitches that fit within the respective ranges of these singers.

EXAMPLE 4.1 - VOICE RANGES

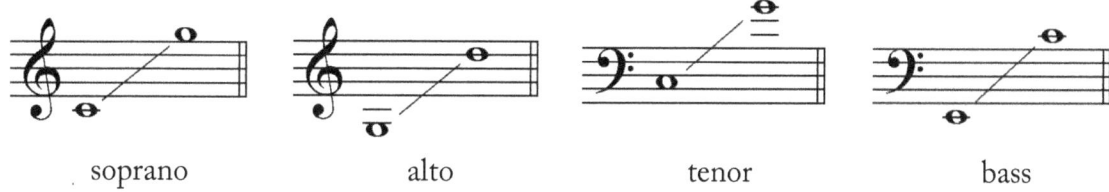

soprano   alto   tenor   bass

Normally, the voices are written on a grand staff with the soprano and alto voices on the upper treble staff, and the tenor and bass voices on the lower bass staff. We can easily take an example of piano voicing in close spacing such as we wrote in chapter 2 and transform it to chorale style writing.

VOICING IN FOUR PARTS WITH CLOSE SPACING

Below is a short melody in G major with Roman numerals indicating the harmonies.

EXAMPLE 4.2 - MELODY WITH ROMAN NUMERAL HARMONIZATION

G: I   IV   I   V   I

In example 4.3 below, the harmonies have been realized using piano voicing in close spacing:

EXAMPLE 4.3 - MELODY HARMONIZED IN CLOSE POSITION PIANO VOICING

G: I   IV   I   V   I

In example 4.4 below, the excerpt is rewritten for four voices. The upper two notes of the chord voicing in the right hand are placed on the upper staff as the soprano and alto voices. The lowest voice of the right hand as well as the root-tone pitch for the left hand are placed on the lower staff as the bass and tenor voices. Notice that the notes used are the exact same as those used in the piano voicing version of example 4.3, but it is much easier to see how the pitches are performed by four separate singing parts and how they lead to one another in a linear, horizontal manner.

Example 4.4 - Melody Harmonized in Four Parts

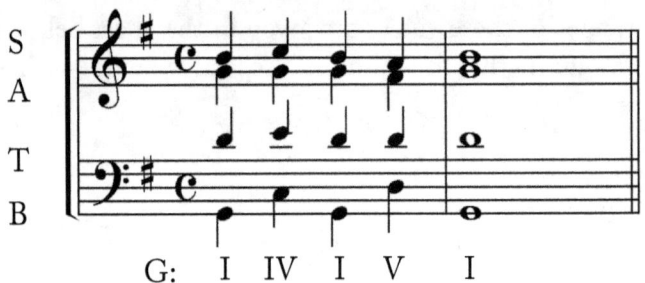

The S, A, T, B letters to the left of the staff refer to the voices: soprano, alto, tenor, and bass. The soprano line is written with stems going up to differentiate it from the alto that has the stems going down. The tenor and bass are differentiated in a similar manner. Notice that in piano voicing, the grand staff is grouped together with a brace on the left hand side ({) indicating that all notes are to be played by one instrument. In the four-part chorale style example, the grand staff is grouped with a bracket on the left ([ ), indicating that different voices or instruments are performing the parts.

Now that we have seen an example of chorale voicing, we can refine our definition of close spacing:

Close spacing is when the distance between the soprano and tenor voices is less than an octave.

Check Your Understanding 4.1

Take the piano voicing excerpt in example 1 below and rewrite it immediately to the right with four-voice close position voicing.

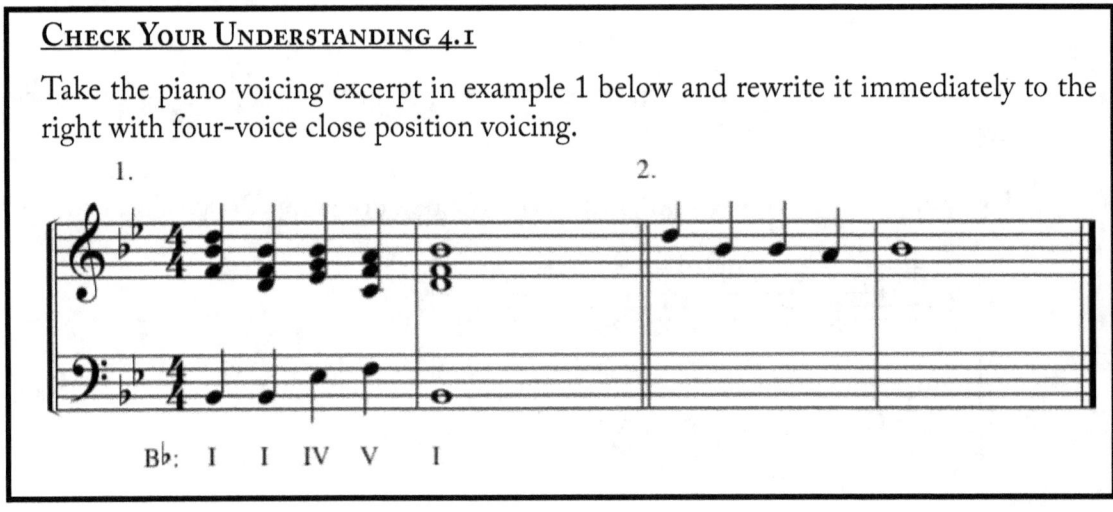

Voicing In Four Parts with Open Spacing

It is also possible to write in chorale style without using close spacing, and for this, we need another definition:

Open spacing is when the distance between the soprano and tenor voices is an octave or greater.

Examine the following closely-spaced harmonization written in piano voicing:

Example 4.5 - Melody with Piano Voicing in Close Spacing

C: I   IV   I   V   I

It would be problematic to transform this directly into chorale style in close spacing. The second harmony (the IV chord) has the pitch A as the lowest note of the right hand part, and this is the pitch that would become the tenor voice in chorale style. By recalling the ranges at the beginning of this chapter, it is apparent that this pitch is above the range of the tenor. To place this harmonization into chorale style, it is best to "spread out" the harmony notes; that is, to use open spacing.

Here is one method for creating open spacing. Look at the first chord in example 4.5 (the I chord) and notice that the notes of the C triad (C, E, and G) in the right hand are as close together as possible. To "open them up," start by writing the melody pitch E and move down to the next closest harmony tone C. However, do not write this tone. Instead, skip it and write the next closest harmony tone below it – the G. Continue in this manner by skipping the chord pitch E and writing the pitch C. Notice that you have written every note of the triad, but they are more spread out:

Example 4.6 - The Process for Creating Open Spacing

Write the chord tones from top to bottom, starting with the melody note, but skip every other available chord tone.

If we rewrite this in four-part chorale style, it will look like the example below. Notice that the distance between the soprano and the tenor is greater than an octave.

Example 4.7 - Chord Voicing in Open Spacing

Here is the same process with the second harmony of example 4.5, the IV chord.

Example 4.8 - Chord Voicing in Open Spacing on the IV Chord

Rewritten in four-part chorale style

If we rewrite the entire example in open spacing, it looks like this:

Example 4.9 - Complete Harmonization in Open Spacing

C: I   IV   I   V   I

You should play this example on the piano and also sing it with a group of vocalists. The open spacing creates a pleasing effect that is quite distinct from close spacing. For this reason, open spacing is used to create variety in the sonority of the music. Also, it is very useful when the melody pitch is written so high that close spacing would pull some of the voices out of their natural ranges.

You should take note of the following important features of example 4.9, as they will become guiding principals in all of your harmonization work:

1. The spacing definitions only apply to the upper three voices. The bass voice is written to create a strong bass line using roots of the chords, and we do not consider it when determining the type of spacing. (Because we are using only root position chords for now, the bass will always be the root tone. However, this will change when we introduce inversions in chapter 9).

2. The vertical distance between the soprano and the alto never exceeds an octave in either open or close spacing. This is also true of the vertical distance between the alto and the tenor. Another way to state this is that when examining the upper three voices, the vertical distance between any two adjacent voices never exceeds an octave. Notice that this is not true of the distance between the tenor and the bass. This vertical distance can have great variety, sometimes as large as a twelfth.

3. The melody is found in the highest voice, the soprano, and the other tones are written beneath.

4. All chords are complete; that is, they contain the root, third, and 5th of each chord.

5. Because we are using three-note chords in a four-part voicing style, one of the pitches will necessarily appear twice. This is called the **doubled pitch**. For root position chords, this doubled pitch will always be between the bass and some other voice. You should look at example 4.9 and find all the doubled pitches.

6. You will find that if the harmony is changing to a new chord, the voice that is doubled with the bass is never the same twice in a row. For example, in the first chord the bass is doubled with the tenor, but in the second chord, the bass is doubled with the soprano. You should verify this fact throughout example 4.9.

Check Your Understanding 4.2

Take the piano voicing excerpt in example 1 and rewrite it immediately to the right with four-voice open position chords. The first voicing is done for you.

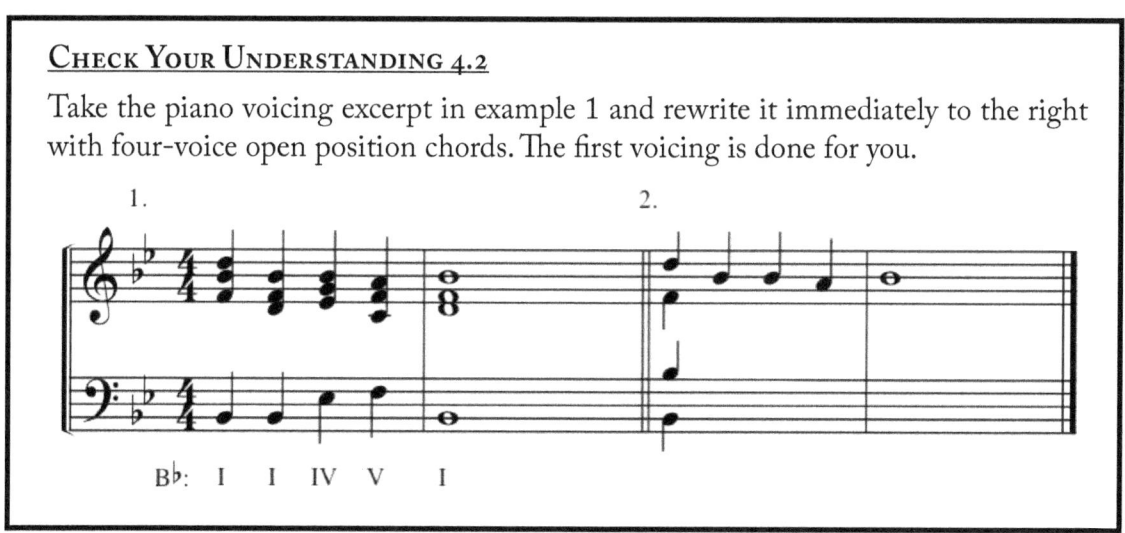

EXERCISE 4.1: For each example, notate the triad indicated by the chord symbol by writing a **root position** chord in four-part, **closely spaced** chorale style. The soprano note is given. You should fill in the alto, tenor, and bass using proper stem directions. The first example is done for you.

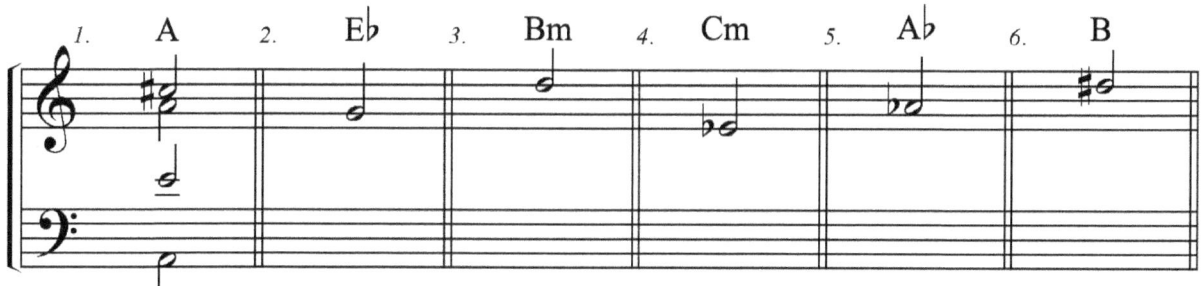

EXERCISE 4.2: Do the same for these examples, but use **open spacing**.

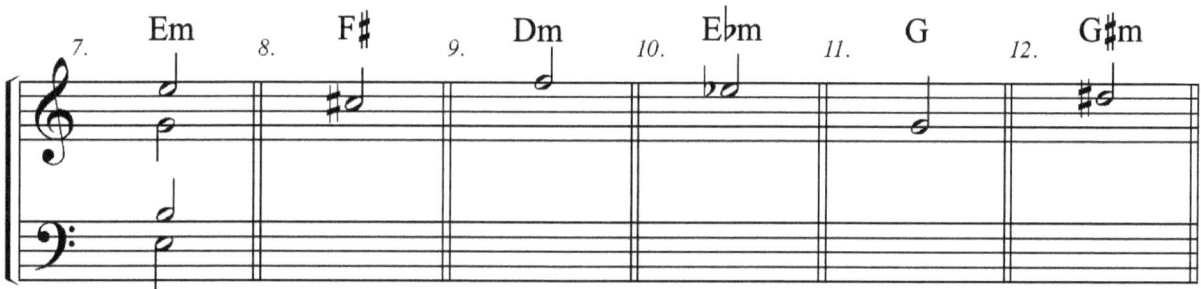

EXERCISE 4.3: For each example, write the key signature and then the harmony of the indicated Roman numeral. Use four-part chorale style in **close spacing** and in **root position**. The soprano note is given, and the first example is done for you.

Key of D: vi   Key of g: iv   Key of d: V   Key of F: I   Key of e♭: V

EXERCISE 4.4: Do the same for these examples, but use **open spacing**.

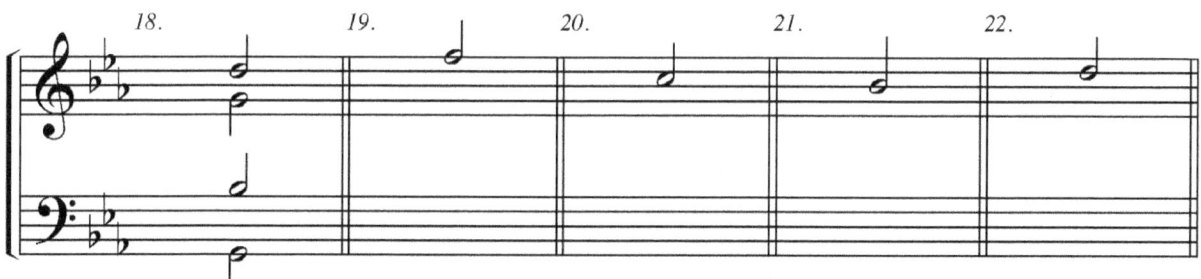

Key of E♭: iii   Key of A♭: IV   Key of f: V   Key of g♯: III   Key of B♭: vi

Exercise 4.5: Fill in the alto, tenor, and bass notes under the given soprano melody. Use proper stem directions. For this first example, write all the chords in **root position** and in **close spacing**. The first chord has been completed.

F: I I IV V I I V   I I IV I V V I

Exercise 4.6: Fill in the alto, tenor, and bass notes under the given soprano melody. Use proper stem directions. For this example, write all the chords in **root position** and in **open spacing**. The first chord has been completed.

A: I V I I IV I V   I V I I IV V I

Exercise 4.7: Fill in the alto, tenor, and bass notes under the given soprano melody. Write all chords in **root position**. Start by writing the chords in **open spacing**. Switch to **close spacing** where indicated and continue in close spacing to the end. The first chord has been completed.

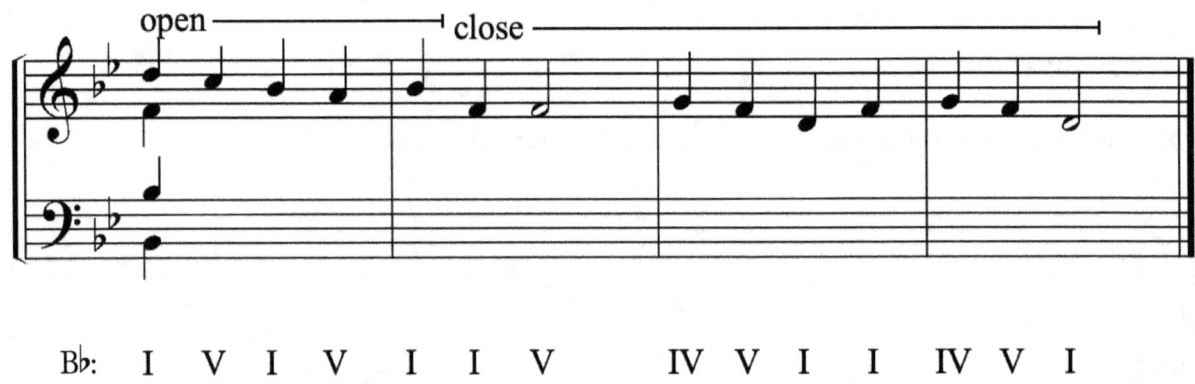

B♭: I V I V I I V   IV V I I IV V I

Chapter 5: Voice Leading and Forbidden Parallels

> **TERMS AND CONCEPTS IN THIS CHAPTER**
>
> | | | | |
> |---|---|---|---|
> | parallel motion | doubled voice | forbidden parallels | consecutive 5ths by |
> | similar motion | melodic leaps | parallel 5ths | contrary motion |
> | contrary motion | harmonic interval | parallel octaves | overtones |
> | oblique motion | crossed voices | parallel unisons | fundamental |
> | no motion | | | |

THE FOUR TYPES OF MOTION

Motion in music refers to the changing of pitch levels in the melodic lines. There are four classifications for motion when describing music written in two or more parts: parallel, similar, contrary and oblique. **Parallel motion** involves two lines moving in the same direction that retain the same interval number (Ex. 5.1 a). **Similar motion** is also when the moving lines are in the same direction, but the interval changes (Ex. 5.1 b).

EXAMPLE 5.1 - PARALLEL AND SIMILAR MOTION

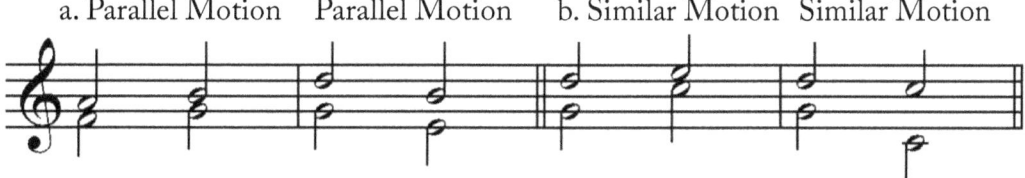

Contrary motion (Ex. 5.2a) involves lines moving in opposite directions, and **oblique motion** (Ex. 5.2b) is when one note is stationary and the other moves.

EXAMPLE 5.2 - PARALLEL AND SIMILAR MOTION

If the rhythm is moving along in music but the pitches do not change, then we say that there is **no motion**.

EXAMPLE 5.3 - NO MOTION

It is possible to examine the types of motion present in a four-part chorale setting by looking at the relationship between any two voices. For example, we could determine the type of motion between the soprano and alto, the soprano and tenor, the soprano and bass, the alto and tenor, the alto and bass, or the tenor and bass. For the following example, examine the motion between the soprano and bass.

Example 5.4 - "Old 100"

Motion between the soprano and bass:

P = parallel
S = similar
C = contrary
O = oblique
NM = no motion

As shown above, there is great variety in the different types of motion in a chorale, and contrary motion is quite prevalent between the voices.

General Characteristics of Four-Part Chorale Style Voice Leading

Examine example 5.4 again (the hymn is often referred to as "Old 100") and answer the following questions:

1. Is each chord complete?
2. Which chord tone is doubled in each chord?
3. Which voice seems to have the widest and most frequent leaps?
4. Which voices seem to have the smallest and least frequent leaps?
5. What is the largest leap you see in the alto or tenor voice?
6. What is the largest harmonic (vertical) distance between any two adjacent voices (soprano – alto, alto – tenor, tenor – bass)?
7. Which chords are in close spacing and which are in open spacing?
8. Are all the voices within their respective ranges?
9. Does the order of the voices (top to bottom) ever change? In other words, is soprano always the highest? Are the alto, tenor and bass always underneath the soprano and in that order?
10. What does the time signature seem to be?

Here are some important part-writing rules that can be derived from your observations:

- Use all **complete chords**.
- **Double the root tone of all root position triads**.
- Alto and tenor lines should be mostly smooth and stepwise. **Keep the melodic leaps in the alto and tenor lines to a minimum, and never larger than a fourth.**
- **The harmonic interval between adjacent voices should be an octave or less.** This only applies to the upper three voices and not to the distance between the bass and the tenor, which can be larger.
- Use a **variety of chord spacings**.
- Use a **variety of different types of motion**.
- Keep the voices in their respective ranges and maintain their respective order from top to bottom. In other words, **avoid crossed voices**.

Below is a part-writing example that has several mistakes, as listed below.

Example 5.5 - Part Writing Example with Mistakes

Part-writing mistakes for Example 5.5:

1. Crossed voices. The tenor is higher than the alto.
2. Alto and tenor voices are not smooth enough. The alto and tenor voices should be mostly stepwise. There are too many leaps in these voices from beginning to end.
3. Melodic interval is too large in the tenor. The tenor from chord 2 to chord 3 skips the interval of a fifth. The alto and tenor should not skip more than a fourth. Also, the harmonic interval between the alto and tenor is too large.
4. Melodic interval is too large in the alto. Also, this is an incomplete chord. The chord is missing the 5th.
5, 6. No mistakes
7. Crossed voices. The tenor is higher than the alto. Also, the bass is below its normal range.

5.1. Check Your Understanding

In the example below, you should identify as many part-writing mistakes as you can.

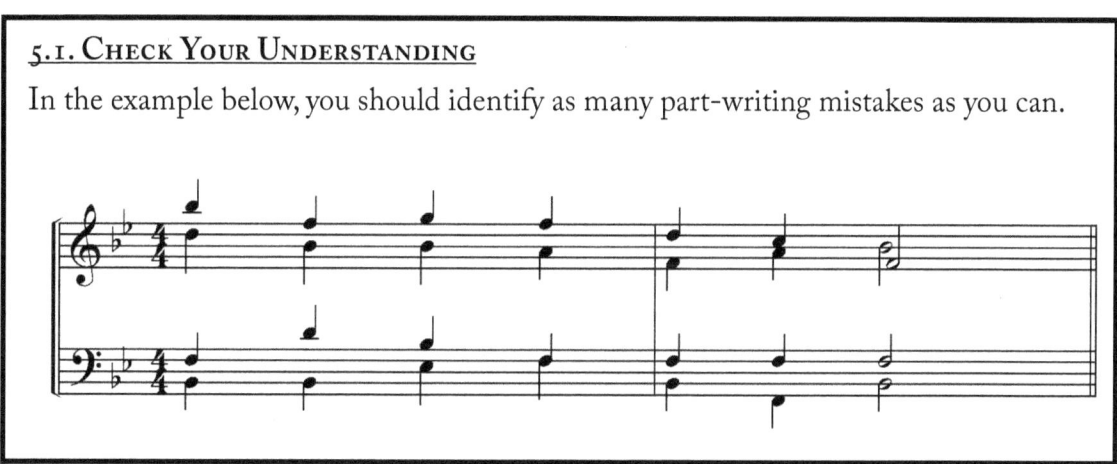

Forbidden Parallels

There is an additional principle of chorale part writing that is a bit more difficult to discern but equally important to the style. This involves the special avoidance of certain parallel perfect intervals.

If the interval of a harmonic perfect 5th appears between any two voices, it will never appear between those same two voices on the next chord if the voices are moving. In other words, we will rarely if ever see **parallel 5ths** in any pair of voices.

If the interval of a harmonic unison or octave appears between any two voices, it will not appear between those same two voices on the next chord if the voices are moving. In other words, we will rarely if ever see **parallel 8ves** or **parallel unisons** in any pair of voices.

Parallel 5ths, parallel 8ves and parallel unisons are called **forbidden parallels**. Here are four examples of forbidden parallels:

Example 5.6 - Forbidden Parallels

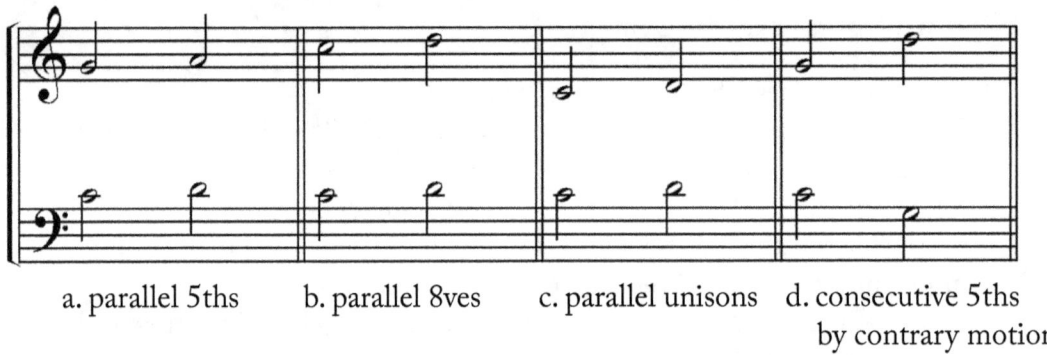

a. parallel 5ths   b. parallel 8ves   c. parallel unisons   d. consecutive 5ths by contrary motion

In a, b, and c above, the restrictions against parallel 5ths, octaves, and unisons have been clearly violated. In the last measure (d. consecutive 5ths), the problem is less clear. The perfect fifth of the first interval moves into another perfect fifth, but by means of contrary motion. Even though this is not exactly the same as a parallel 5th, it should still be avoided. The effect is very similar to that of the parallel 5th, and the sound of consecutive fifths seems to disrupt the independence of the voices.

At this point, it would be helpful to have a more compete explanation of why some parallel intervals were avoided throughout much of the common-practice period. You may recall that for every pitch that is sounded by an instrument, a series of **overtones** (higher pitches) are produced. The overtone series is always produced in the same relationship to the **fundamental** (the lowest harmonic – the frequency that is actually perceived as the pitch). The overtone series is shown below as it extends four octaves above the fundamental. The actual overtone series is infinite.

Example 5.7 - The Overtone Series Above C

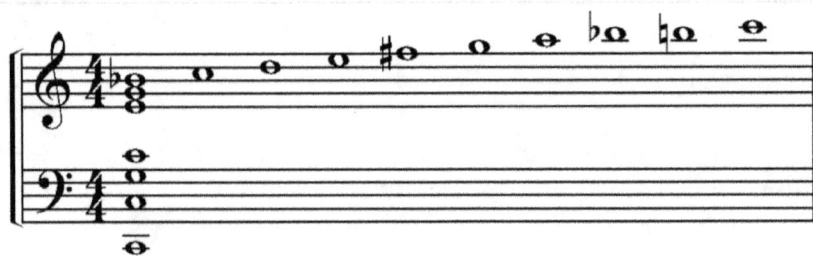

The intervals of the perfect 8ve and the perfect 5th figure prominently in the series as the first and second overtones. Composers have always been keenly aware of the importance of these intervals with regard to their strong harmonic position in the overtone series. In Western European sacred music of the 10th and 11th centuries, composers often harmonized their melodic lines with parallel 5ths in a style called parallel organum. Eventually, composers began searching for ways to create more independence in their lines, as the parallel 5ths sound more like a reinforcement of the overtone series than an actual independent musical line. Toward this end, composers of the 15th century began to take special care to avoid parallel 5ths, octaves, and unisons. They considered this practice to be rather ancient and devoid of melodic independence.

It is important to realize that it is not necessary or desirable to avoid all parallel intervals. Here are a few examples that are perfectly acceptable:

Example 5.8 - Some Examples of Allowable Motion

a. parallel 6ths   b. parallel 4ths   c. unequal 5ths   d. no motion

A variety of parallel intervals aside from 5ths and octaves are allowable, as seen in example a and b above. While the parallel 4ths in example b would be unusual in two-part writing, it would be prevalent in three and four-part writing. Example c (unequal 5ths) shows an example that seems to be parallel 5ths, but on closer inspection, only the second interval is a perfect 5th. It is possible to have part writing where a diminished 5th moves into a perfect 5th, or vice versa. In example d, the pitches are not moving at all, so there is no voice-leading problem. Since there is no motion, the two consecutive perfect fifths in a row are entirely allowable.

Here is a short part-writing example with some forbidden parallels.

Example 5.9 - Part Writing Example with Forbidden Parallels

Eb: I   I   IV   V   I

To find the forbidden parallels in example 5.9, isolate all the possible pairs of voices and then examine the intervals in those pairs.

Example 5.10 - Isolating the Soprano with the Alto and the Tenor Voices

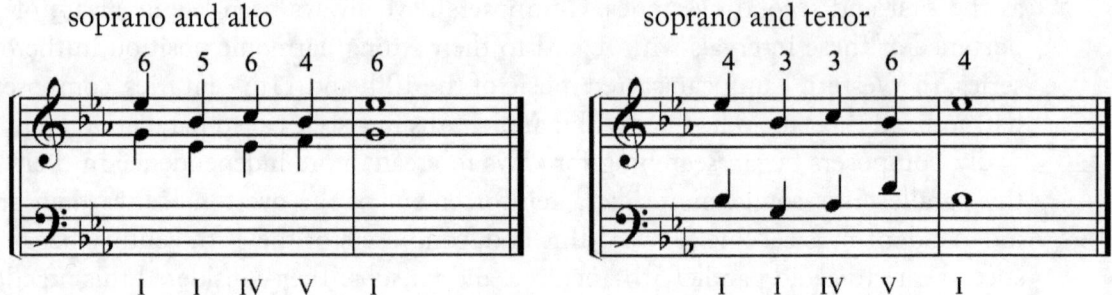

There are no problems with these pairs since we never see two 5ths, 8ves or unisons in a row. Notice that if the interval is a compound interval (greater than an octave), we reduce it to its simple equivalent (less than an octave) when naming it.

Example 5.11 - Isolating the Soprano with the Bass Voice

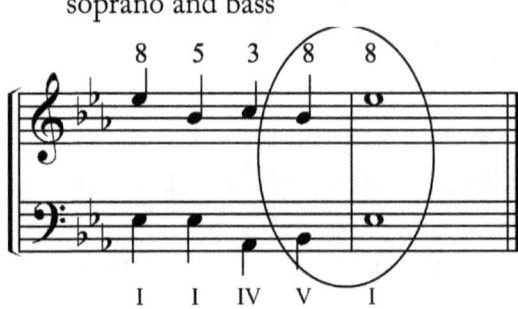

In this pair, there is a parallel interval problem. The last two chords (the V going to I) have parallel 8ves between the soprano and bass.

Complete your search for forbidden intervals by examining the remaining pairs. Label the intervals and circle any parallel 5ths, 8ves, or unisons.

Example 5.12 - Isolating the Remaining Voice Pairs

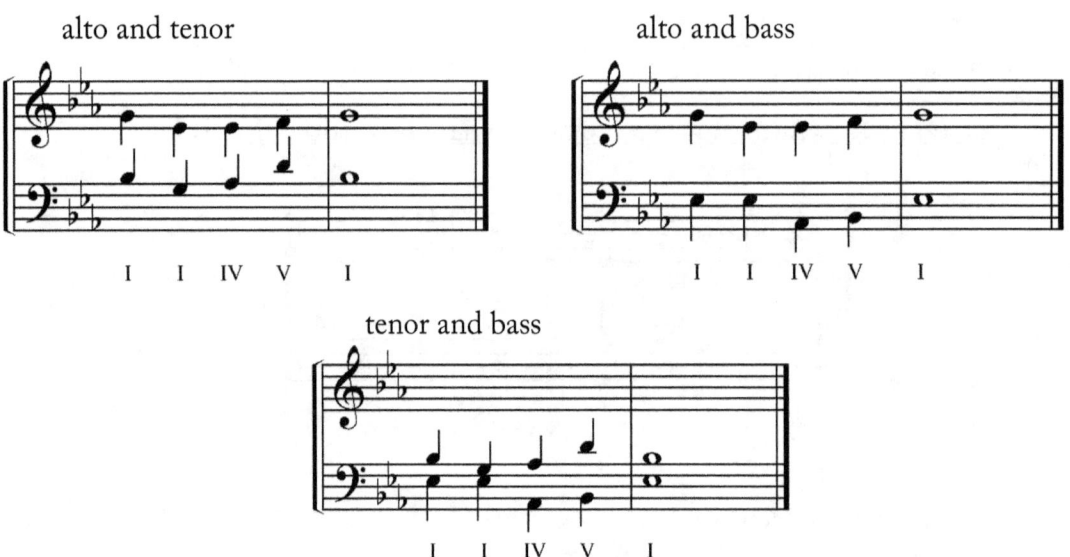

CHECK YOUR UNDERSTANDING 5.2

Find one instance of parallel 5ths and one instance of parallel 8ves in the following example.

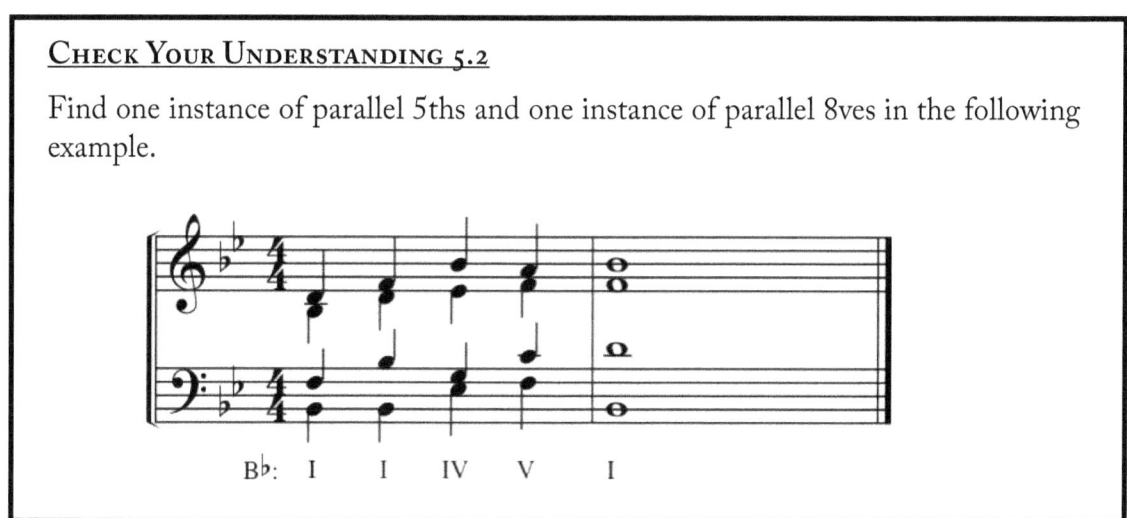

DIRECT 5THS AND 8VES

Direct 5ths and 8ves present a voice-leading problem that is similar in nature to the forbidden parallels discussed above. These are special cases where the interval of the 5th or 8ve is presented in a stark, unmusical fashion with awkward voice leading. In particular, we consider the approach to the 5th or 8ve too stark if all the following are true:

1. The 5th or 8ve is between the bass and the soprano voice, and
2. The approach to the 5th or 8ve is by similar motion between the bass and the soprano voices, and
3. The approach to the 5th or 8ve involves a skip (interval greater than a 2nd) in the soprano voice.

EXAMPLE 5.13 - DIRECT 8VES AND DIRECT 5THS

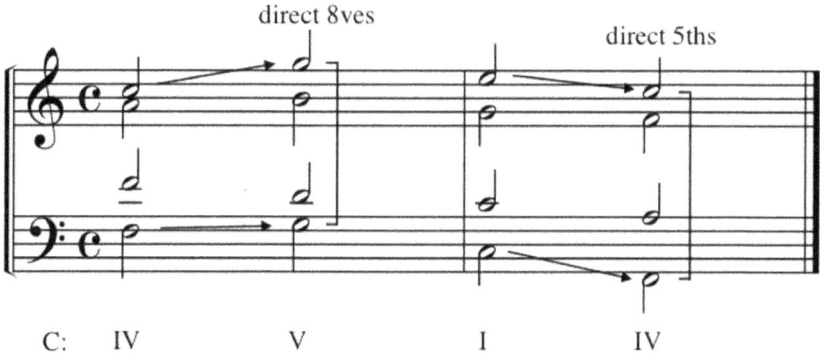

Exercise 5.1

Find one example of the following mistakes in the chorale below.

1. Parallel 5ths
2. Parallel 8ves
3. Consecutive parallel 5ths by contrary motion
4. Vertical spacing too large
5. Direct 5ths
6. Direct 8ves
7. Crossed voices
8. Voice outside of its range
9. Incomplete chord
10. Incorrect doubling
11. Melodic (horizontal) leap too large

Circle each mistake in the music and label it.

Chapter 6: Progression and Voice Leading with I, IV, V

> **TERMS AND CONCEPTS IN THIS CHAPTER**
>
> | | | |
> |---|---|---|
> | harmonic functions | plagal cadence | root tone motion |
> | tonic | half cadence | up a 2nd |
> | dominant preparation | antecedent - consequent | down a 5th |
> | dominant | perfect cadence | forbidden melodic intervals |
> | authentic cadence | imperfect cadence | augmented 2nd |
> | | | tritone |

HARMONIC FUNCTION

The primary chords, I, IV, and V, represent the fundamental **harmonic functions** in tonal music. The I chord, or **tonic**, is the defining harmony of a key. It is quite often the starting chord as well as the chord to which the music returns. We can think of it as the "home" harmony of the composition.

The IV, or subdominant, is an excursion away from home. It may return back to the tonic, but it is also very likely to lead us on to the dominant. For this reason, we will place it in a more general and functional category called **dominant preparation**.

The V, or **dominant**, also represents an excursion away from tonic. Being built a perfect 5th above tonic, it has a special relationship to the tonic based on its relationship to the strong second overtone of the tonic overtone series. However, it also has a certain instability due to its prominent tendency tone, the leading tone, which is the chord third of this harmony. Since the leading tone is only a half step away from tonic, it has a strong tendency to return to tonic. For this reason, the dominant is most often used to take advantage of this tension to create a strong progression back to tonic.

EXAMPLE 6.1 - THE OVERTONE SERIES AND THE DOMINANT CHORD

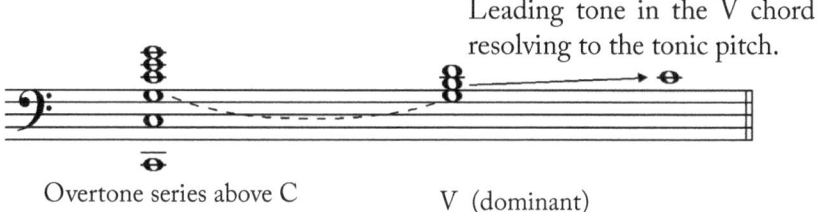

The harmonic functions in tonal music can be summarized as follows:

EXAMPLE 6.2 - THE HARMONIC FUNCTIONS

Tonic	Dominant Preparation	Dominant	Tonic
I	IV	V	I
This is the "home" harmony. It can progress to any other chord.	The IV chord can either return to tonic or progress to dominant.	The V chord progresses strongly back to tonic.	The progression ultimately returns to tonic.

AUTHENTIC, PLAGAL, AND HALF CADENCES

A phrase is a musical sentence with a distinct melodic shape. The end of a phrase can be perceived by some kind of cessation of forward motion as well as a distinct harmonic formula. This melodic and harmonic destination at the end of a phrase is called the **cadence**. In the chorale excerpt by J. S. Bach below, there are two phrases with a cadence at the end of each.

Example 6.3 - Two Cadences in a Chorale by J. S. Bach

In these phrases, we can perceive then ends of the phrases (the cadences) because there is a cessation of the forward motion by means of a fermata. In both cadences, the harmony consists of a very strong progression of the V chord (dominant) resolving to the I chord (tonic). When the V chord resolves to the I chord at the end of a phrase, we call this an **authentic cadence**.

The next example is a simple arrangement of the "Ode to Joy," the famous theme from the last movement of Beethoven's Ninth Symphony. In this excerpt there are two clear, four-measure phrases. The cadences can be easily perceived because of the longer half-note rhythm at the end of each.

Example 6.4 - Half and Authentic Cadences in Beethoven's Ode to Joy

The first cadence (in measure 4) is considered "non-final" because the V chord keeps us in anticipation of the second phrase. In fact, any cadence that does not end on a I chord is considered non-final. When a phrase specifically ends with a V chord, as in the cadence in m. 4, it is called a **half cadence**.

The second phrase ends with a much more "final" sound by using the authentic cadence, V to I. Phrases that are paired in this manner, with the first ending on a half cadence and the second ending on an authentic cadence, are referred to as **antecedent – consequent**, or question – answer phrases.

There is one more variety of the final cadence called the **plagal cadence**. It is most often seen at the end of church hymns, as shown in the example below.

<u>Example 6.5 - Plagal Cadence</u>

The plagal cadence is the progression IV going to I, and because it concludes with the I chord, we can say that it falls into the category of a final cadence. However, it does not have the same strength as an authentic cadence. In fact, it is not common to see it functioning independently in common-practice music. As you can see in the example above, the hymn seems to conclude with the strong authentic cadence (V – I), and then the plagal cadence is used on the word "Amen" almost as an afterthought.

The cadences we have seen up to this point can be summarized as follows:

<u>Example 6.6 - Summary of Cadences</u>

Final Cadences		Non-Final Cadence
Authentic Cadence	Plagal Cadence	Half Cadence
V - I	IV - I	ends on V

Perfect and Imperfect Cadences

One additional distinction made among final cadences (authentic and plagal) is whether they are **perfect** or **imperfect**. A perfect cadence is one that would provide a strong and satisfactory effect at the conclusion of a composition. In order for a final cadence to be called perfect, both chords of the cadence must be in root position, and the final pitch of the soprano must be the tonic pitch. If either of these conditions is not met, the cadence is called imperfect.

Below are examples of perfect cadences:

Example 6.7 - Perfect Cadences

Perfect Cadence:
1. Both chords are in root position.
2. In the last chord, the soprano is on the tonic pitch.

Check your Understanding 6.1

Here are examples of **imperfect cadences**. Why are they imperfect?

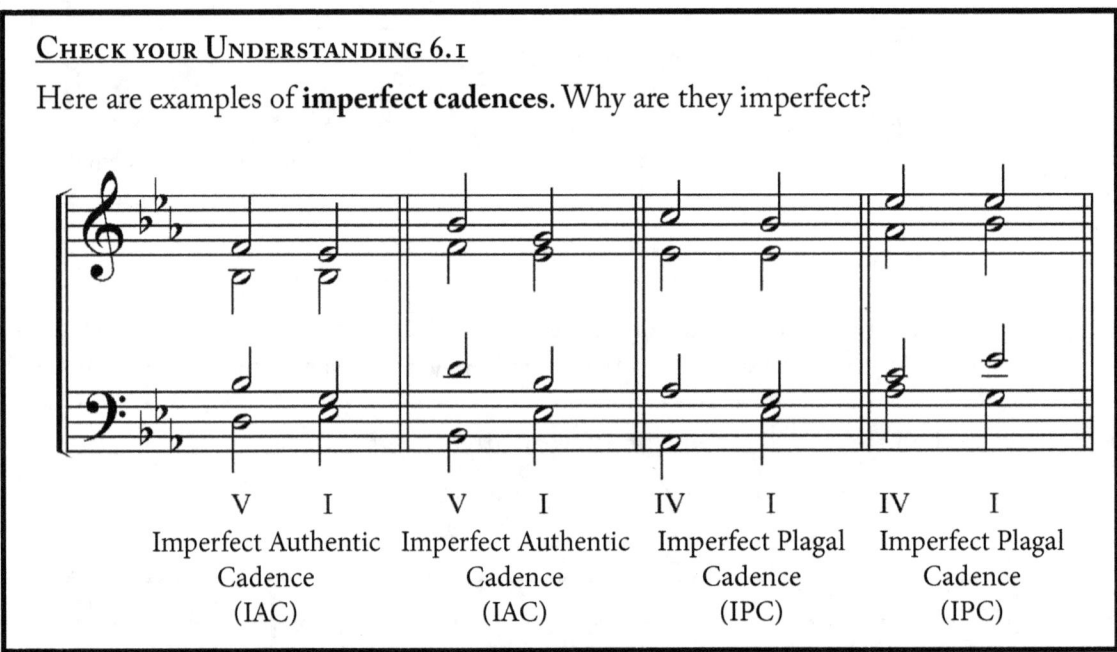

Root Tone Motion

To help generalize procedures and concepts when voice-leading chords, we classify progressions according to their **root tone motion**. In order to keep the classification system simple and useful, root tone motions are limited to three types, those of the second, the third, and the fifth. For example, if a IV chord moves to V chord, we say that the root tone motion is a "up a second." Similarly, if a V chord moves to a IV chord, we say that the root tone motion is "down a second." When I moves to IV, the motion is called categorized as "down a fifth."

The root tone motion designation is the theoretic distance that the root moves, not necessarily the actual distance found in the bass line. For instance, motion from I to V is called root tone motion "up a fifth," regardless of whether the actual bass line is moving down a 4th or up a 5th. The progression of I to IV is called "down a fifth" even if the actual bass tone is moving up a fourth. In this way we can limit the total number of root tone motion categories to three: the second, third, and fifth.

Below are several examples of root tone motion in seconds and fifths.

Example 6.8 - Root Tone Motion in Seconds and Fifth

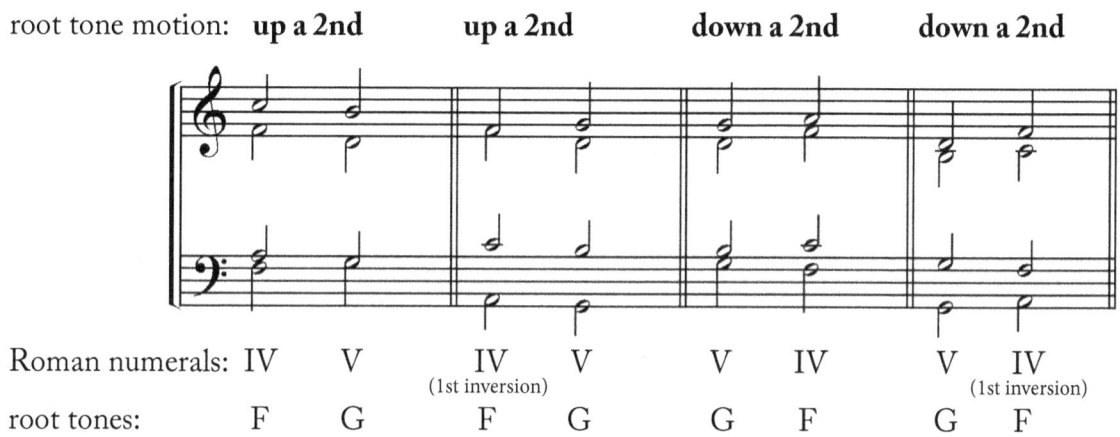

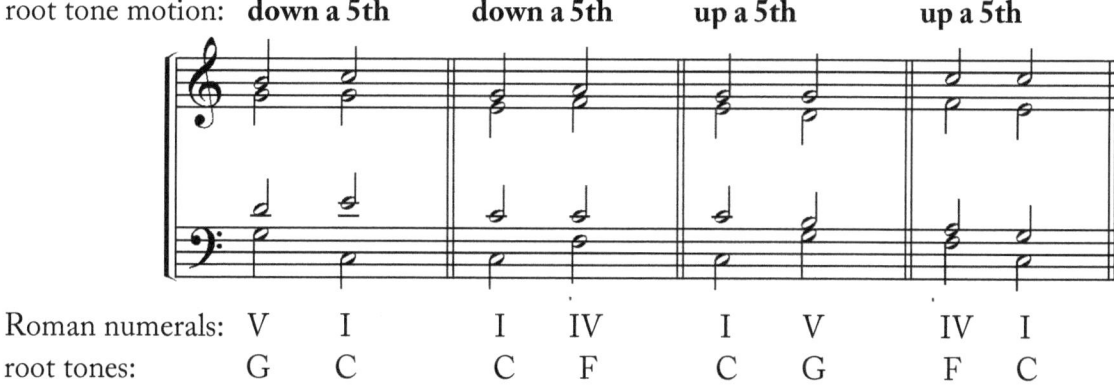

Voice Leading Procedures for Root Tone Motion in 5ths

- For root position progressions moving by the **root tone motion of the fifth**:
- Keep the root tones in the bass voice.
- Find a common tone that can be retained in one of the upper three voices.
- Move the remaining two voices stepwise into chord tones that produce complete chords with proper doubling (doubling of the bass).

For example, when moving from a I chord to a V chord in the key of G, we will follow this procedure to create good voice leading, as shown below in Example 6.9:

Example 6.9 - Following the Root Tone Motion in 5ths Procedure

Voice-lead a I chord going to a V chord in the key of G:

1. Write a root position I chord using either open or close spacing. Make sure to <u>double the bass tone</u>.
2. Begin to write the following V chord by placing the root in the bass.

Note that both chords are in root position, and the root tones are written in the bass.

3. Identify the common tone that exists between the I chord (the G major triad: G-B-D) and the V chord (the D major triad: D-F♯-A). As you can see, the common tone is the pitch D.

4. Since the common tone D was written in the tenor for the I chord, place it in the <u>same voice</u>, the tenor, for the V chord.

5. Move the remaining voices <u>stepwise</u> to complete the second triad, and make sure to use proper doubling (<u>double the bass pitch</u>).

Here is another example of voice leading in a progression involving root tones moving in 5ths with I going to IV in the key of A:

Example 6.10 - Voice Leading I to IV in the Key of A Major

The common tone is A

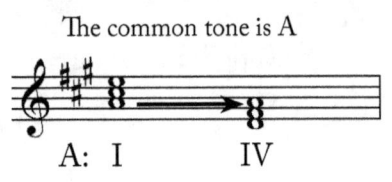

Common tone in the same voice

Root tones in the bass, and the bass tone is doubled in both chords

Check Your Understanding 6.2

Complete these two harmonization examples using the method outlined above for voice leading progressions that involve root tone motion in 5ths.

Voice Leading for Root Tone Motion in 2nds

When moving from one chord to another involving the root tone motion of a second, there are no common tones involved. It is important to take special care in avoiding parallel 5ths and parallel 8ves, and this is achieved by using **contrary motion**.

For root position progressions moving by the **root tone motion of the second**:
Keep the root tones in the bass voice.
Move the upper three voices contrary to the bass.

To illustrate, here is a progression from IV to V in the key of E♭.

Example 6.11 - Following the Root Tone Motion in 2nds Procedure

There are no common tones when moving from the IV chord (A♭-C-E♭) to the V chord (B♭-D-F) in the key of E♭, as is always be the case when moving by root tone motion of the 2nd.

1. Voice the IV chord in root position and make sure to double the bass.
2. Begin to write the V chord by placing the root tone (B♭) in the bass.

3. Move the upper three voices (soprano, alto, and tenor) contrary to the bass. In this example, the bass is ascending stepwise, so move the upper voices downward to the next nearest chord tones of the V chord. Make sure that the bass is doubled.

Check Your Understanding 6.3

Complete these two harmonization examples using the method outlined above for voice leading progressions that involve root tone motion in 2nds.

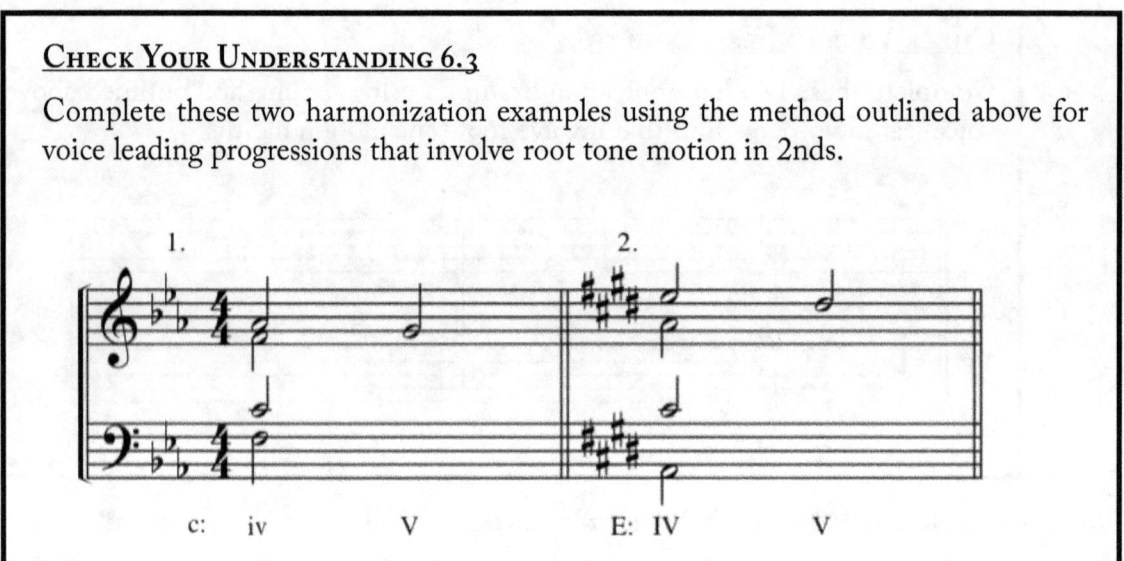

Forbidden Melodic Intervals

When moving from iv to V in a minor key, follow the same rules as outlined above for root tone motion of the second. It is especially important to be careful with this progression in minor because it presents the possibility of a forbidden melodic interval – the augmented 2nd. As already discussed in chapter 3, special care must be taken to raise the leading tone when writing V or vii° chords in a minor key. This adjustment to the harmonic minor key (the raising of scale degree 7) presents a potential melodic problem that may appear whenever progressing into or out of the V or vii° chord. Take another look at the harmonic minor scale:

Example 6.12 - The Augmented 2nd Interval in the Harmonic Minor Scale

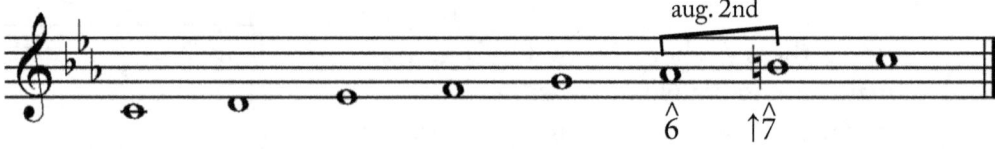

The interval from scale degree 6 to the raised scale degree 7 is an augmented 2nd. This interval is very hard to sing and is generally avoided in part-writing. One more interval that is also difficult to sing and should be avoided as a melodic interval is the tritone (aug 4th or dim. 5th), and this interval can be found between scale degree 4 and scale degree 7 in both major and minor keys.

When voice-leading, avoid writing the melodic interval of either the aug 2nd or the tritone in any of the voices. These are **forbidden melodic intervals.**

You can see from the example below, that the interval of the augmented 2nd becomes a potential problem when progressing from iv to V:

EXAMPLE 6.13 - POTENTIAL AUGMENTED 2ND IN A MINOR KEY PROGRESSION

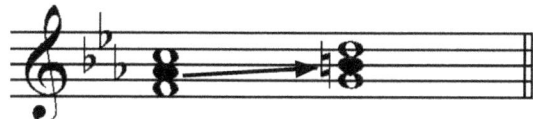

In progressions moving from iv to V, there will be no problem with augmented 2nd intervals in any of the voices as long as you use the voice leading rule for root tone motion in seconds: move the upper voices contrary to the bass when root tone motion is the second.

EXAMPLE 6.14 - AVOIDANCE OF AUGMENTED 2ND INTERVAL

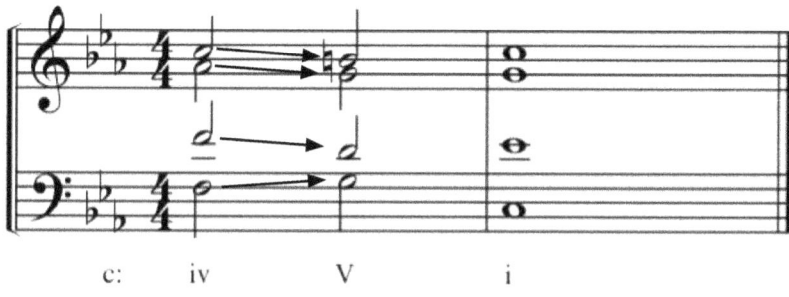

c: iv   V   i

Upper three voices (soprano, alto, and tenor) moving contrary to the bass.

Exercise 6.1

For the following examples, first identify the key (they are all major keys). Then, determine the type of root tone motion and fill in the second chord according to the rules given in chapter 6. Label each pair as a cadence by using one the following designations: PAC (perfect authentic cadence), IAC (imperfect authentic cadence), PPC (perfect plagal cadence), IPC (imperfect plagal cadence), or HC (half cadence). The first example has been completed for you.

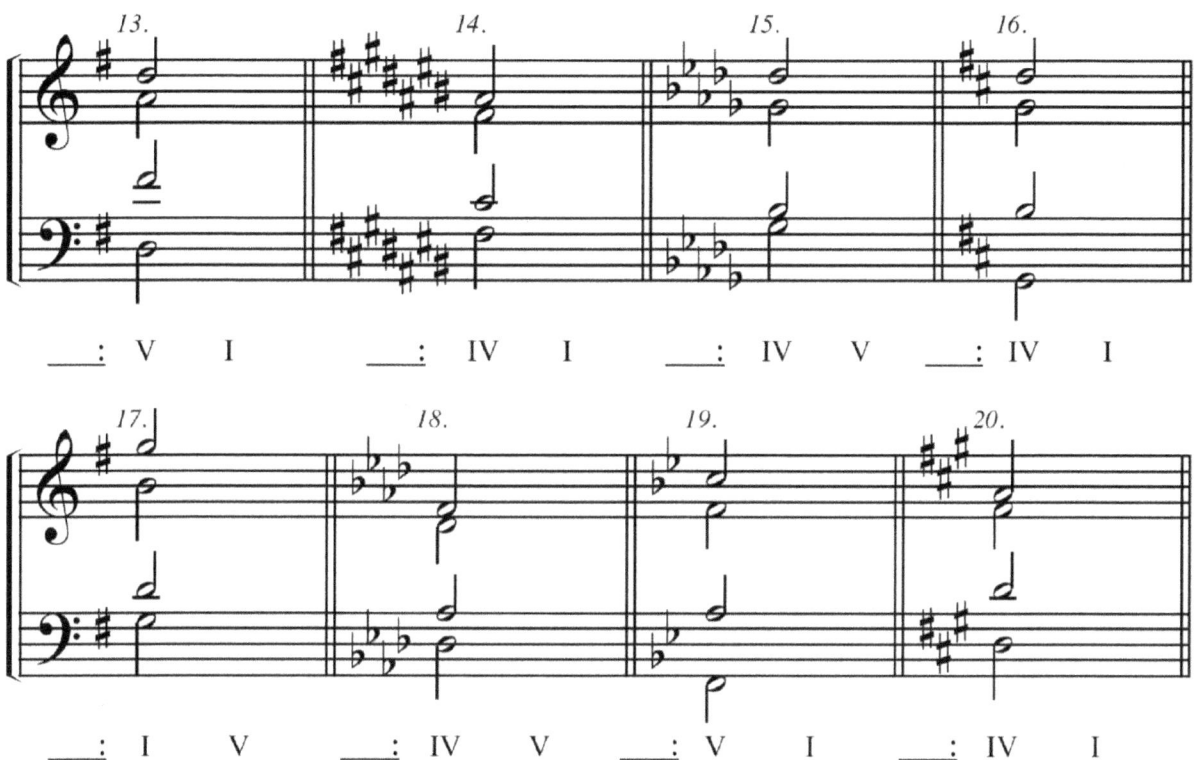

Exercise 6.2

For each example, first identify the key (they are all minor). Then progress from iv to V using good voice leading. The first one is done for you.

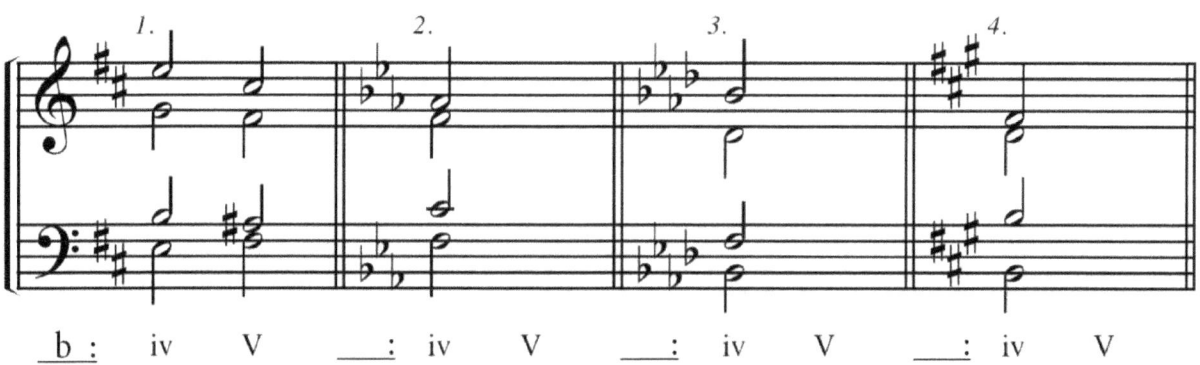

Exercise 6.3

For each example, look at they key and determine what the second chord should be based on the given soprano. Write in the Roman numerals and the pitches of the second chord. Do not write a key signature, but make sure to include all necessary accidentals. The first example is done for you.

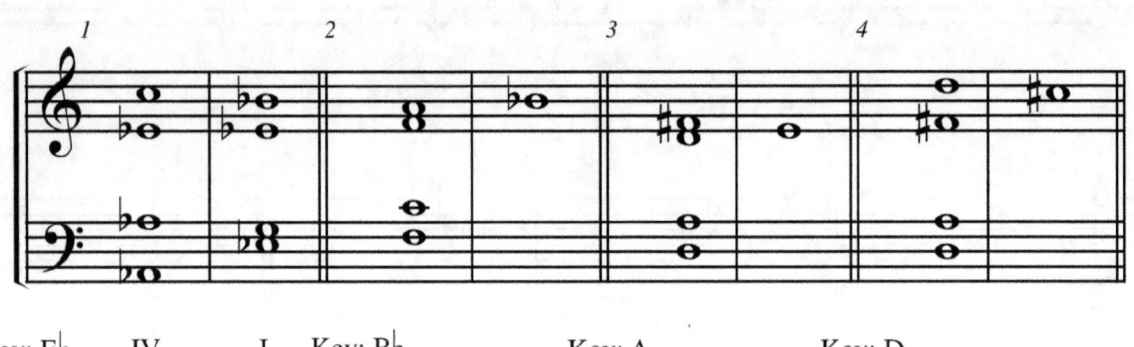

Key: E♭   IV   I   Key: B♭   Key: A   Key: D

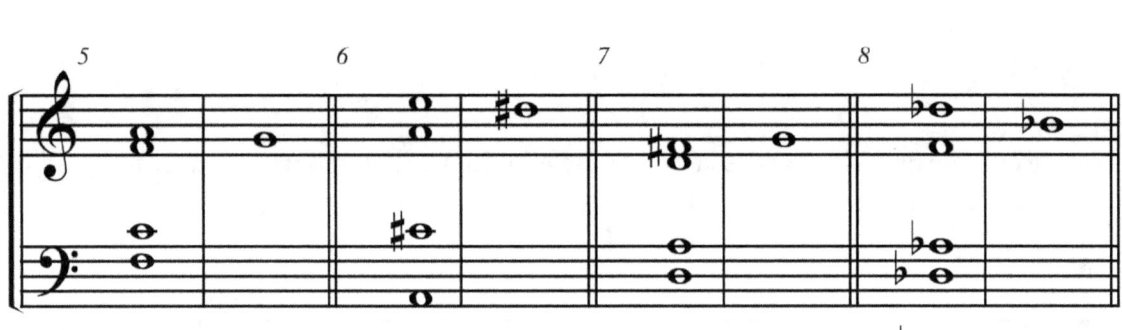

Key: F   Key: E   Key: G   Key: A♭

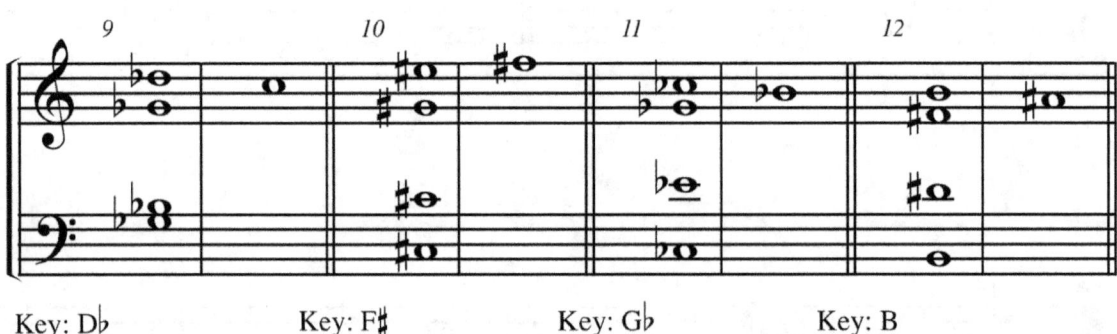

Key: D♭   Key: F♯   Key: G♭   Key: B

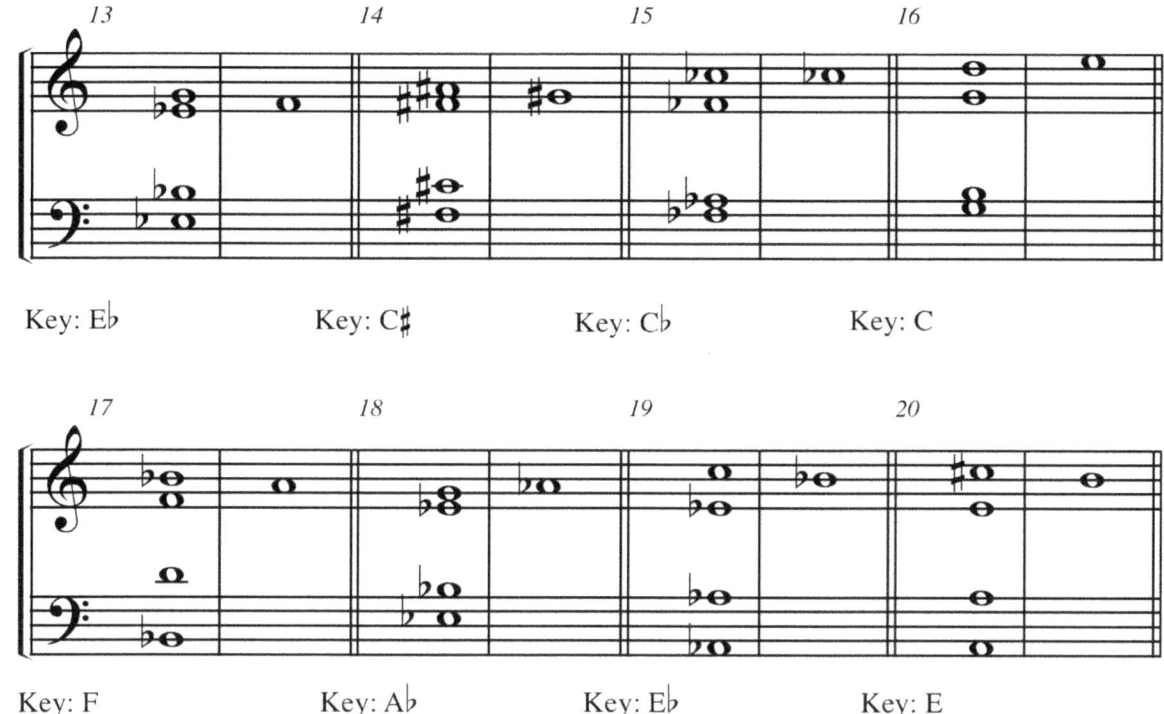

Exercise 6.4

Harmonize these melodies by adding the alto, tenor, and bass. Use only **root position, primary chords** (I, IV V for the first example and i, iv, V for the second example). If "close" is indicated, use close spacing. If "open" is indicated, use open spacing.

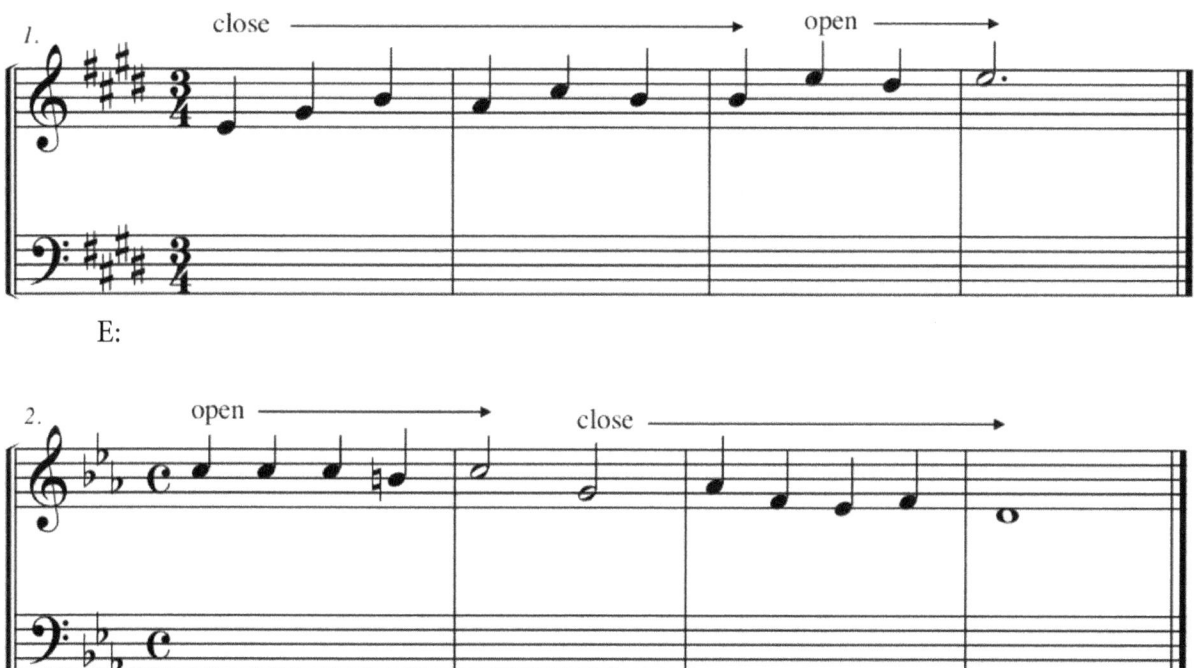

Exercise 6.5

For this example, harmonize in four parts using the Roman numerals indicated. Start in close spacing, but switch to different spacings as necessary.

Key of G: I   I   V   V   I   I   IV   IV   I   I   IV   V   I

Exercise 6.6

Complete these harmonizations using i, iv and V chords. Use the indicated spacings. Label all cadences.

1.

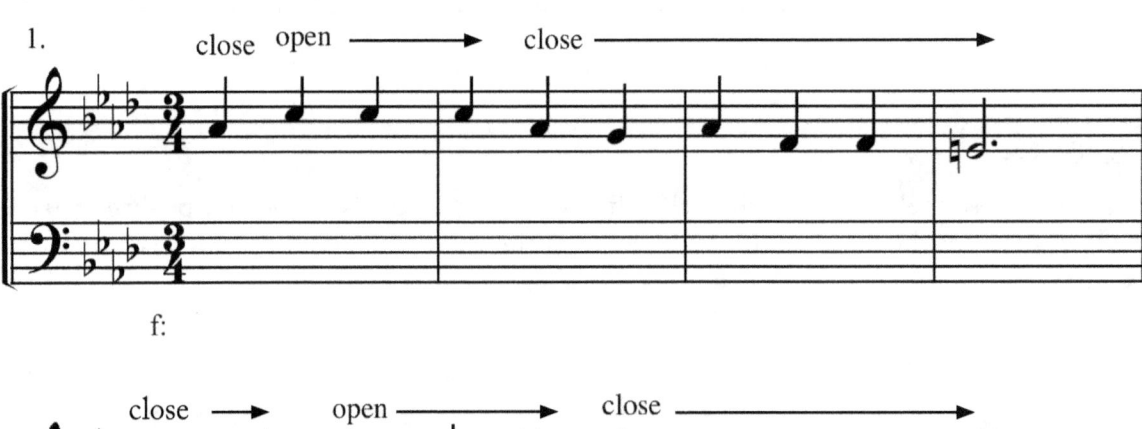

f:

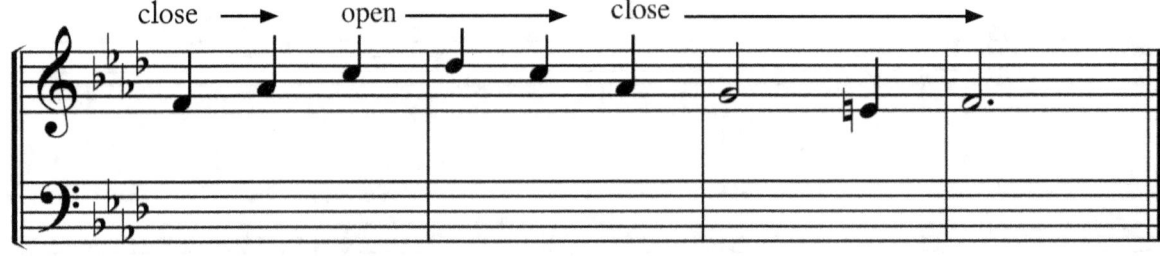

2.

f♯:

Exercise 6.7

Complete this harmonization using the harmonies indicated. Label all cadences. Start in open spacing, but change the spacing as necessary.

50

Chapter 7: Harmonizing Melody: More Considerations

> TERMS AND CONCEPTS IN THIS CHAPTER
>
> harmonic rhythm   retrogression   root tone motion in 5ths
> forbidden parallels   overlapped voices   alternate voice leading

CHOOSING HARMONIES

When choosing the specific harmonies for a simple chorale-style melody, there are often many choices for each melody note, as shown in the two-phrase example below:

EXAMPLE 7.1 - HARMONIC CHOICES

One good approach is to settle on the harmonies for the cadences first. As you can see, there are two choices at the first cadence (measure 4), either a plagal cadence (IV to I) or a half cadence (IV to V). Because plagal cadences are rather rare, especially without the support of a strong authentic cadence preceding it, we will choose the half cadence. For the second cadence (measure 8), the choices are either an authentic cadence (V to I) or a rather unusual non-final cadence (V to IV). Clearly, the typical authentic cadence is the better choice.

The following example is a completed harmonization of the melody in example 7.1, but be forewarned, several weak choices have been made.

EXAMPLE 7.2 - HARMONIZATION WITH MISTAKES

There were several issues that were mishandled in example 7.2:

1. Harmonic rhythm. When the music moves into a new measure, the harmony should usually change. This helps the listener to perceive the metric organization of the rhythm.

2. Forbidden parallels. There are parallel 5ths between the bass and the tenor as well as parallel 8ves between the bass and the soprano. Whenever you choose a harmony that results in the exact same note in the bass as is in the soprano, parallels will result.

3. Harmonic rhythm. By repeating the IV harmony on beats 2 and 3, greater emphasis has been placed on beat 2, resulting in a syncopated harmonic rhythm. In this style, such harmonic syncopation should be avoided. In other words, the preferable place to change the harmony in common time is beat 3.

4. Harmonic rhythm. This is the same problem as in #1.

5. Retrogression. Although retrogression is permissible, it should not be too prevalent. In this case, V should progress to a tonic function and should not regress to the IV chord, which has a dominant preparation function.

6. Unclear function. This is a rather meandering and aimless progression, as the chords seem to move back and forth between IV and V.

7. and 8. Forbidden parallels. There are parallel 5ths between the bass and soprano as well as parallel 8ves between the bass and alto. Be careful not to create parallel 5ths with the melody when choosing the harmonies.

9. Forbidden Parallels. The perfect 5th interval between the bass and soprano on the V chord moves to another perfect 5th interval between the bass and soprano on the I chord. Although the voices move in contrary motion, the perfect 5ths are still consecutive, and this is considered to be an error. We call this "**consecutive 5ths by contrary motion.**"

10. Harmonic rhythm. It is best to change the harmony going into beat 3. The repetition of the same chord on beats 2, 3, and 4 places extra emphasis on beat 2, resulting in syncopation of the harmonic rhythm.

11. Overlapped Voices. The tenor voice on the V chord (the pitch A) moved to a lower pitch than the bass voice on the previous beat (B♭). This kind of overlapping confuses the integrity of the order of the voices. (Overlapped voices will be covered more thoroughly in chapter 9.)

These are the main concepts covered above:

Forbidden Parallels. This includes parallel perfect 5ths or 8ves between pairs of voices. Even if these intervals are consecutive but approached by contrary motion, it is still forbidden.

Harmonic Rhythm. The metric stresses created by the placement and pattern of harmonies within the measure. Special care should be made so that the beginning of the measure can be perceived by means of a chord change. Also, syncopation of the harmonic rhythm by placing undue stress on the second beat in common time should be avoided.

Retrogression. Harmonic motion that is contrary to the normal tendency of the chord function. V to IV is considered retrogression because, normally, IV (dominant preparation) progresses to V (dominant).

Below is an example of the same melody with a much better harmonization:

EXAMPLE 7.3 - IMPROVED HARMONIZATION

Note that the harmonic rhythm is much improved in this harmonization. The harmony always changes at the beginning of the measure, and there is no syncopated harmonic rhythm causing undue emphasis on beat 2. In fact, there are several instances where the same harmony is used for beats 1 and 2 and also for beats 3 and 4.

CHECK YOUR UNDERSTANDING 7.1

For each exercise below, add a good Roman numeral harmonization

ALTERNATIVE VOICE LEADING METHODS FOR ROOT TONE MOTION IN 5THS

You should notice that in example 7.3, there are several instances where alternative voice leading procedures have been used for root tone motion in 5ths. These locations are marked as "1," "2," and "3" in the music and explained below. The alternative voice leading comes about by either a special demand of the melody note or because of a change of spacing.

Alternate voice leading used for root tone motion in fifths in example 7.3:

1. Do not retain a common tone and move upper three voices in the same direction. This was necessary because the potential common tone in the soprano of the I chord moved to the 3rd of the IV. Since we cannot change the melody, an alternative voice leading was necessary.

2. Retain a common tone and move the 3rd of the first chord into the 3rd of the second chord in the same voice. In this case, the melodic motion in the soprano did not allow for a small melodic interval in the tenor. This is a typical solution when there is a change of spacing.

3. Do not retain a common tone and move upper three voices in the same direction. Again, the melodic motion in the soprano demanded some alternative voice leading.

Check your Understanding 7.2

Complete these harmonization examples using an alternative and appropriate method of voice leading for root-tone motion in 5ths.

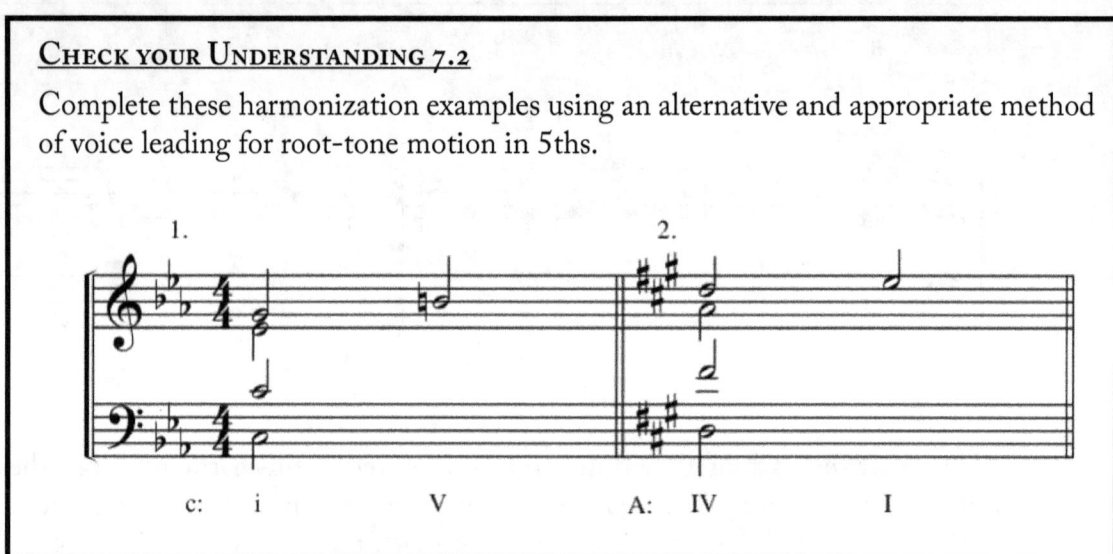

Exercise 7.1

Complete these examples by using an alternative voice leading method: do not retain a common tone and move the upper three voices in the same direction. The first example is done for you.

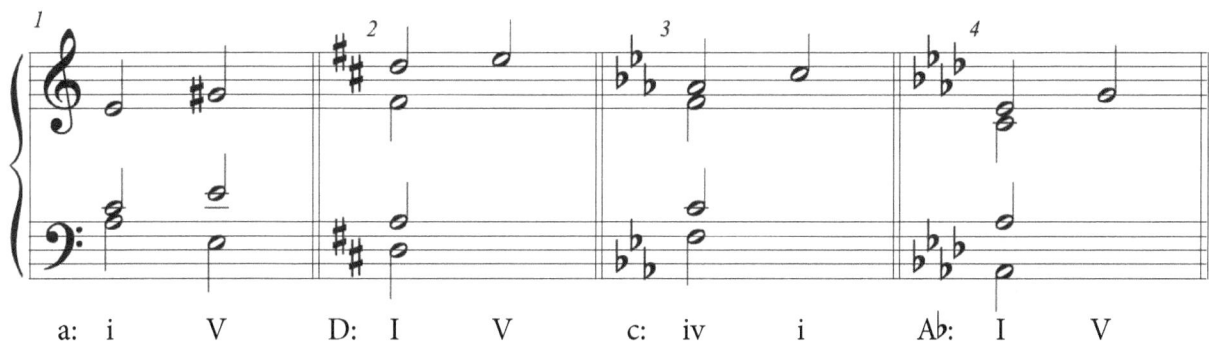

a: i V   D: I V   c: iv i   A♭: I V

f♯: i iv   F: I IV   e: i V   D♭: V I

Exercise 7.2

Complete these examples by using an alternative voice leading method: retain a common tone and move the 3rd of the first chord into the 3rd of the second chord in the same voice. The first example is done for you.

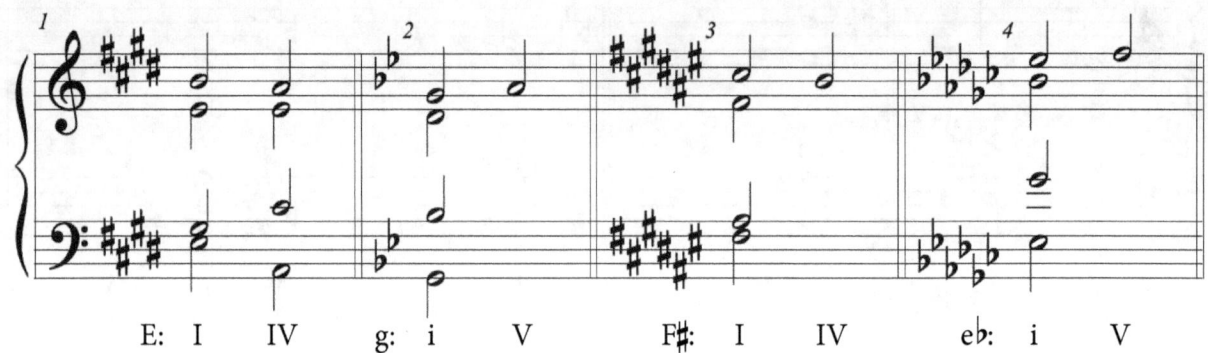

E: I   IV   g: i   V   F♯: I   IV   e♭: i   V

G: V   I   d: i   V   D♭: V   I   b: i   V

Chapter 8: Secondary Triads

> **TERMS AND CONCEPTS IN THIS CHAPTER**
>
> primary triads   dominant preparation function   deceptive cadence
> secondary triads   dominant function   leading tone resolution
> tonic function   root tone motion in 3rds   irregular doubling

TONAL FUNCTIONS OF PRIMARY AND SECONDARY TRIADS

The primary triads are I, IV, V in a major key and i, iv, V in a minor key. The secondary triads are ii, iii, vi, vii° in a major key and ii°, III, VI, vii° in a minor key.

EXAMPLE 8.1 - SECONDARY TRIADS IN THE KEY OF C MAJOR

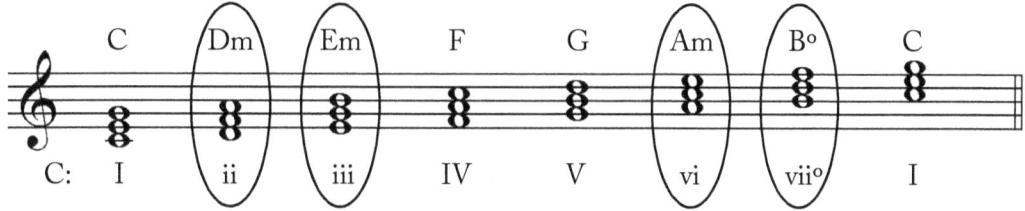

When harmonizing with secondary triads, it is helpful to classify them in terms of their functions, just as we did with the primary triads. In fact, we will use the same three functions for classification: **tonic, dominant preparation, and dominant**.

EXAMPLE 8.2 - TONIC FUNCTION (T)

Both the vi chord and the iii chord share pitches with the I chord, and both could also function as tonic. However, the vi chord is the best secondary chord in this function because it also includes the root tone of the I chord.

EXAMPLE 8.3 - DOMINANT PREPARATION FUNCTION (DP)

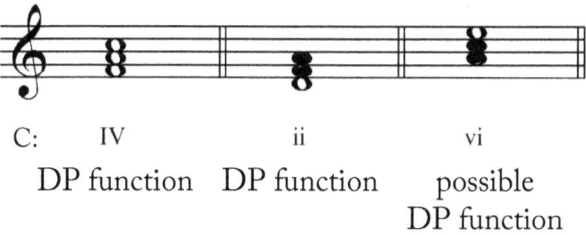

Both the ii chord and the vi chord share pitches with the IV chord, and both could also function as dominant preparation (DP). However, the ii chord is the best secondary triad in this function because it also includes the root tone of the IV chord.

Example 8.4 - Dominant Function (D)

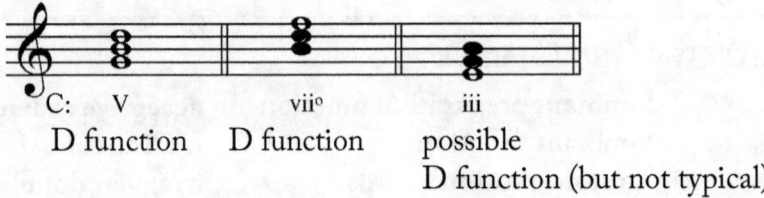

    C: V   viiº   iii
    D function   D function   possible
                                  D function (but not typical)

The viiº chord is the best secondary chord for dominant function. It contains both the important leading tone of the scale as well as another important tendency tone, scale degree 4. Scale degree 4 is only a half step away from scale degree 3 (F – E in this key), and this creates an additional strong pull back to the I chord.

In the chart below, the chord functions are summarized, and the typical progression paths are shown. Notice that motion from a primary chord to its related secondary chord provides additional possibilities for progression.

Example 8.5 - Progression Paths

	Tonic	Dominant Preparation	Dominant	Tonic
primary chords	I	IV	V	I
secondary chords	vi (iii)	ii (vi)	viiº	vi (iii)

Keep in mind that the chart shown in Example 8.5 is only intended to set forth preferences. While it shows the most typical paths of progression, it is not intended to completely restrict other possibilities. Also, keep in mind that it is not unusual for a I chord to move to just about any other harmony.

Root Tone Motion in Thirds

When voice leading with secondary triads, you can use the same root tone motion rules that you used for primary triads. However, one additional type of motion, root tone motion in 3rds, will come into play in progressions such as I to vi, I to iii, IV to ii, and V to viiº. For root tone motion in 3rds, there will always be two common tones, and, if possible, you should retain them as common tones in the same voices. Here is the rule:

For chords moving by **root tone motion of the third**, retain the two common tones in the same voices and move the remaining pitch to the closest tone that will complete the chord.

Example 8.6 - Root Tone Motion in Thirds

    C: I   vi   IV   ii   I   iii

> ### CHECK YOUR UNDERSTANDING 8.1
>
> Complete these harmonizations. Make sure to retain two common tones when progressing by root tone motion in 3rds.
>
>

THE DECEPTIVE CADENCE

The progression V to vi in major as well as V to VI in minor are common progressions that become possible once we begin using secondary triads. As a substitute for the I chord, the vi chord assumes a tonic function, especially when approached from dominant harmony. Also, it may be found at the end of a phrase as a special kind of non-final cadence. Because we are expecting V to resolve to I, it is quite a surprise if it resolves to vi. For this reason, it is called a **deceptive cadence** when found at the end of a phrase.

EXAMPLE 8.7 - DECEPTIVE CADENCE

Faith of Our Fathers (the entire hymn is found in Appendix F)

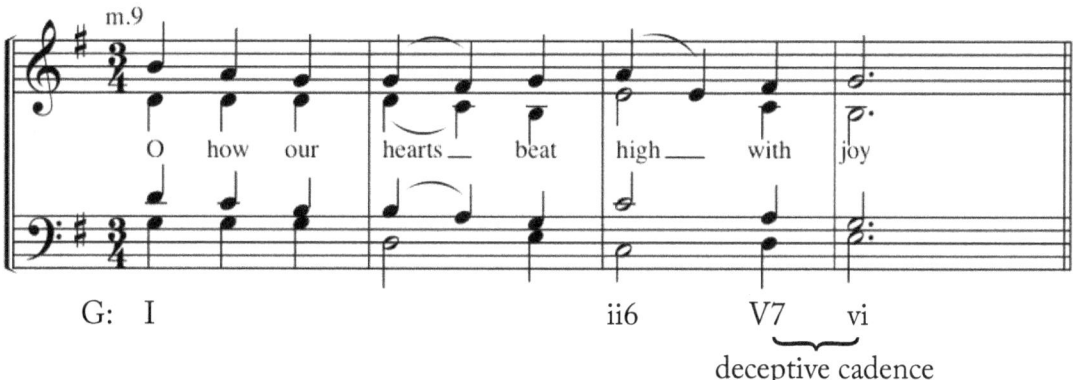

Measure 3 of this example presents a few concepts that we have not yet learned. The ii chord is considered to be inverted because the 3rd of the chord, not the root, is in the bass voice. Also, the V chord is not a triad, but a four-note seventh chord, so named because the distance from the root to highest additional pitch is a seventh interval. Inversions will be covered in Chapter 9, and 7th chords will be covered in Chapter 14. Nonetheless, the last measure of example 8.7 is a good example of a cadence where we are expecting to hear the dominant chord resolve to I, but instead, it progresses to the unexpected vi chord in a deceptive resolution.

When moving from V to vi in a major key, simply follow the rule of root tone motion in seconds by moving the upper three voices contrary to the bass. However, the voice leading of V to VI in a minor key does not seem to work as well when following this rule, as shown in example 8.8 below:

EXAMPLE 8.8 - V TO VI IN A MINOR KEY WITH AUGMENTED 2ND INTERVAL

Actually, there are two reasons why example 8.8 presents poor voice leading. First, the augmented melodic interval (in the soprano) is awkward to sing and should not be written. Second, the leading tone is in an outer voice, and in this position, it has a very strong tendency to resolve upward by half step. **Leading tones, when written in one of the outer voices (bass or soprano) should follow their natural tendency and resolve upward by half step.** Below is another attempt to voice-lead V to VI that includes a good resolution of the leading tone in the soprano.

EXAMPLE 8.9 - V TO VI WITH PARALLEL MOTION

As you can see, the leading tone has been properly resolved, but the preponderance of parallel motion has resulted in both parallel 5ths and parallel 8ves. Below is a third attempt to write good voice leading from V to VI by reintroducing some contrary motion:

EXAMPLE 8.10 - V TO VI WITH TRITONE

While the parallel 5ths and 8ves have been eliminated, careful inspection reveals another forbidden melodic interval, the tritone, in the tenor voice.

Motion from V to VI in a minor key presents a very special problem in voice leading that requires **irregular doubling** to solve satisfactorily. You recall that, normally, we should double the root tone of root position triads, but in this case, we will double the 3rd of the VI chord to avoid the more serious mistakes illustrated above.

Example 8.11 - V to VI with Irregular Doubling of the 3rd

This is the best solution. The doubling is irregular, but we have resolved the leading tone and avoided forbidden melodic intervals and forbidden parallel motion.

When V goes to VI in a minor key, double the third of the VI chord. Do this by resolving the leading tone up by half step and resolving the other voices down (contrary to the bass).

Check Your Understanding 8.2

Complete these deceptive cadences in four voices. Pay particular attention to the doubling of the VI chord.

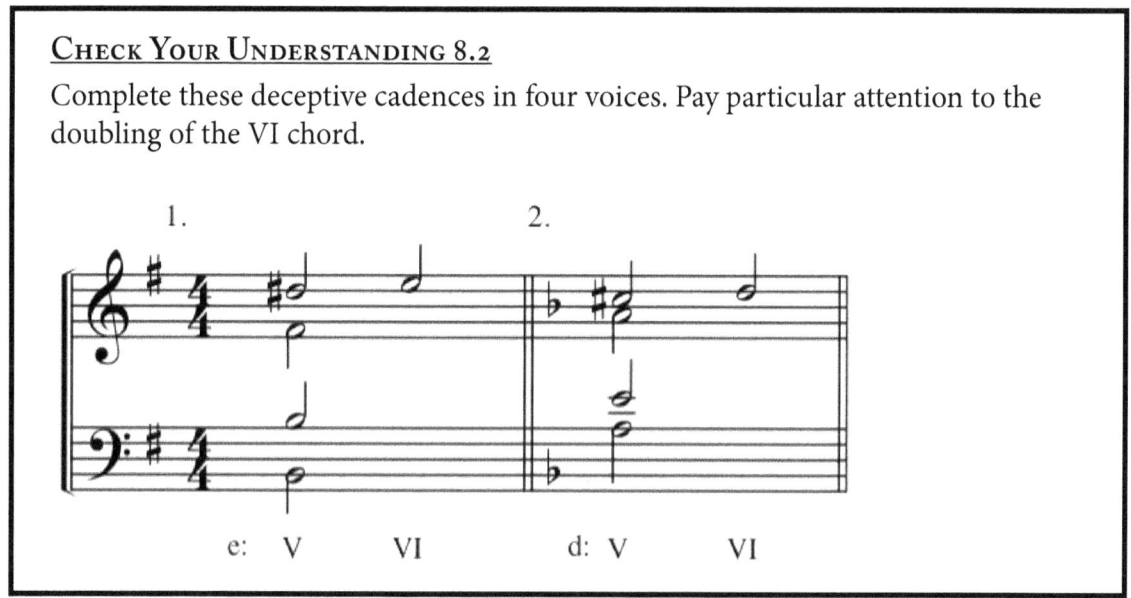

Exercise 8.1

For each example, first identify the key (they are all minor). Then fill in the alto and tenor voices for the V chord. Choose either open or close spacing as appropriate. Finally, voice lead from V to VI. Remember to double the 3rd in the VI chord and write all chords in root position. The first one is done for you.

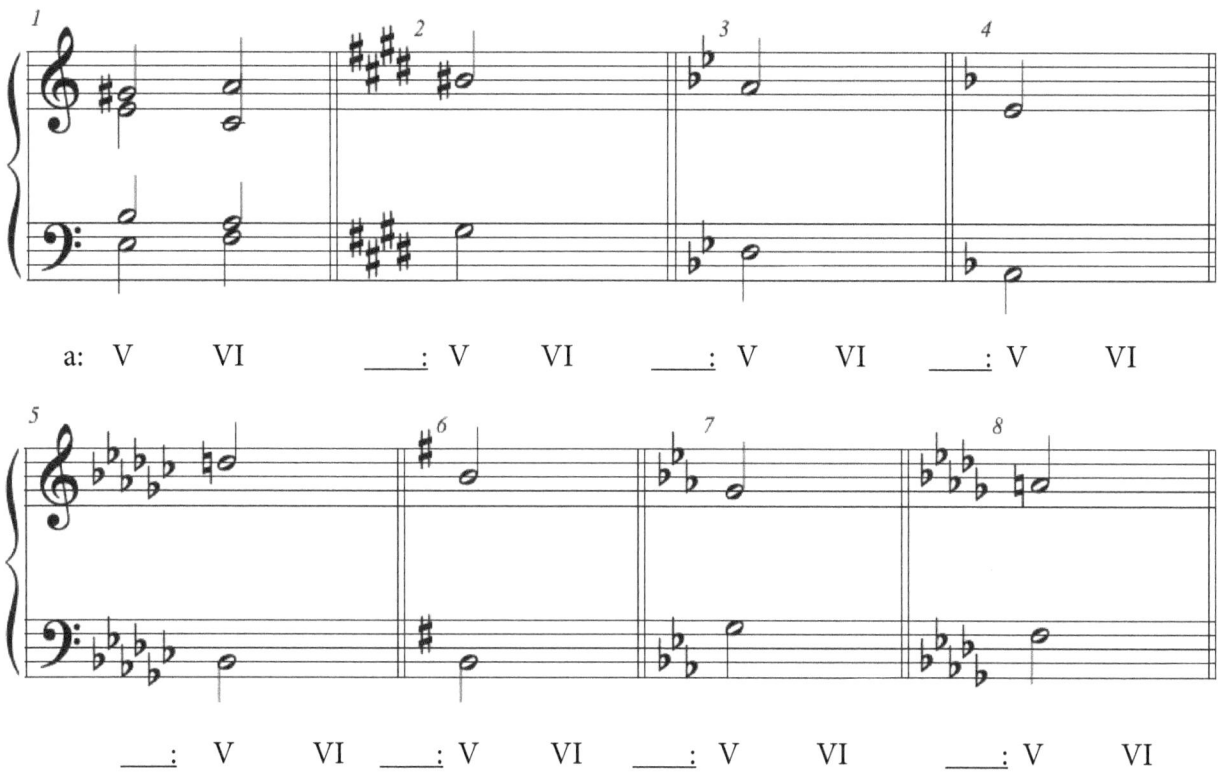

For the following examples, first identify the key (they are all major). Then fill in the alto and tenor voices for the V chord. Choose either open or close spacing as appropriate. Finally, voice lead from V to vi. For this deceptive resolution of V in a major key, it is also best to double the 3rd in the vi chord whenever the leading tone of the V chord is in the soprano. This is so that you can resolve the leading tone upward and avoid parallel 8ves and 5ths.

Exercise 8.2

Fill in the alto and tenor voices. The first example has been done for you.

Exercise 8.3

Harmonize these melodies in four parts. Use only primary triads except where secondary triads are indicated with Roman numerals. Begin each exercise with the suggested spacing. Use only root position chords.

1.

2.
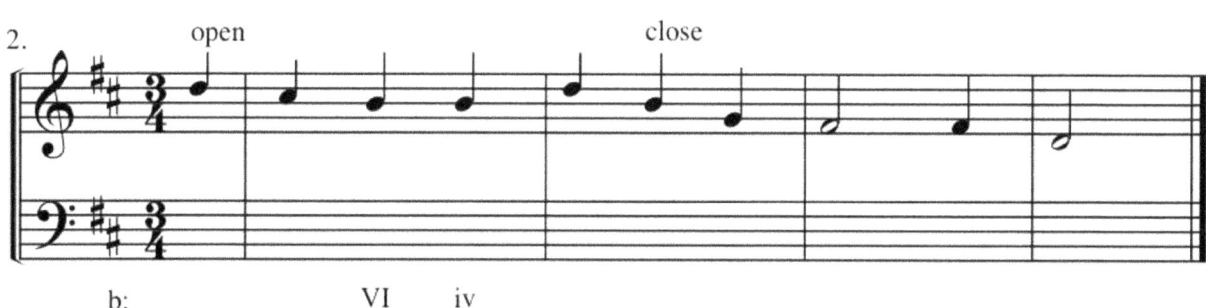

3.

4.

Exercise 8.4

Complete these harmonizations. Use only primary triads except where "sec." is indicated. In those locations, choose an appropriate secondary chord (ii, ii°, iii, III, vi or VI). Use all root position triads.

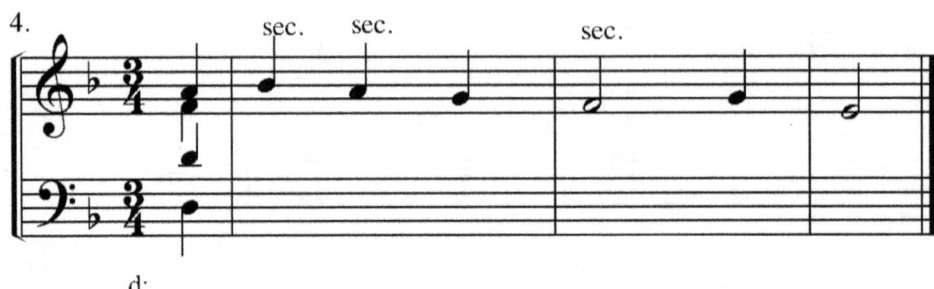

Chapter 9: First Inversion Triads

> **TERMS AND CONCEPTS IN THIS CHAPTER**
>
> first inversion   figured bass   diminished triad doubling
> doubling   overlapped voices   Phrygian half cadence

FIRST INVERSION TRIADS

When triads are inverted in a four-voice texture, it allows the opportunity to use a note in the bass other than the root. This strengthens the harmonization by providing more variety in the sonorities, and also by creating a bass line that is more melodic. When we place only roots in the bass, the triads all have a strong and stable sound, but the bass line is often rather disjunct.

First inversion triads have the **3rd of the chord in the bass.** The upper three voices can contain any of the chord tones, but the 3rd must be in the bass for us to label it as first inversion. Below are a few first inversion chords with the chord degrees labeled:

EXAMPLE 9.1 - EXAMPLES OF FIRST INVERSION TRIADS

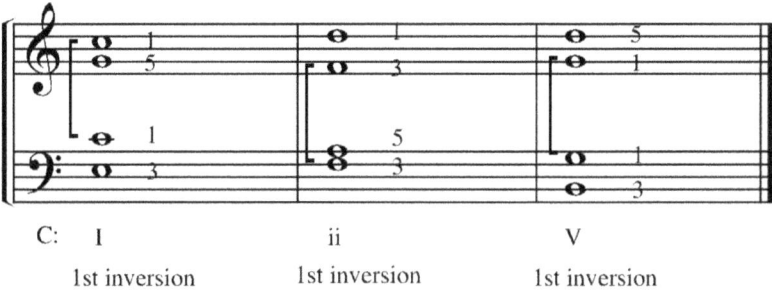

DOUBLING OF FIRST INVERSION MAJOR AND MINOR TRIADS

As you can see in example 9.1, there are a variety of possibilities when it comes to choosing a pitch to double for 1st inversion major and minor triads. In the first chord, the soprano is doubled; in the second chord, the bass is doubled with an inner voice; and in the third chord, the alto and tenor are doubled.

When writing first inversion major and minor triads, the preference is to double the soprano with an inner voice, but other solutions are possible. In all cases, it is forbidden to double the leading tone of the V triad.

LABELING OF FIRST INVERSION TRIADS

Here is an example of a first inversion triad with all the intervals above the bass labeled:

EXAMPLE 9.2 - FIGURED BASS FOR FIRST INVERSION TRIAD

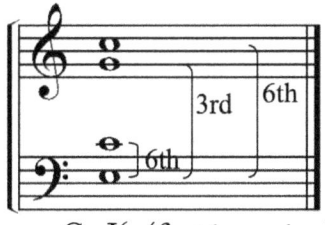

Because all of the intervals are 6ths and 3rds (when reduced to simple intervals), this first inversion I triad can be designated with the notation I$_3^6$ or, more commonly, the shorthand version: I^6

This kind of inversion labeling relates to intervals formed above the bass and is derived from **figured bass notation**. Figured bass is a kind of intervallic shorthand that was commonly written under the bass line in compositions of the Baroque era to give players of chording instruments enough information to improvise their parts.

Usages of First Inversion Triads

There are many instances when first inversion triads can be used to create interesting bass lines. Three examples are given below.

Example 9.3 - First Inversion Usage

In this example, the I⁶ chord creates a kind of arpeggiating motion on the I chord. It also helps the I chord to lead to the IV chord by filling some of the space between the two root tones in the bass.

Example 9.4 - First Inversion Usage

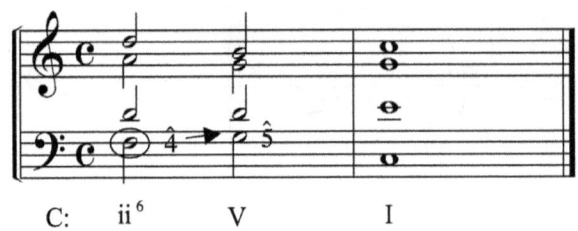

Here, the ii⁶ chord in first inversion emphasizes its dominant function by placing scale degree 4 in the bass. It also allows for smooth stepwise motion into the V chord.

Example 9.5 - First Inversion Usage

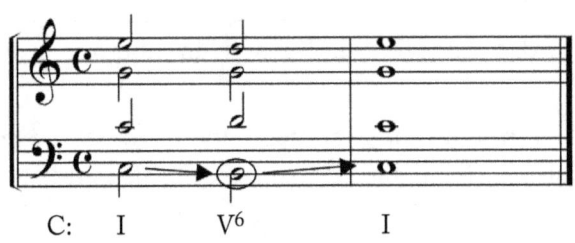

The V⁶ chord in first inversion shown here results in very smooth, neighboring motion, leading from and going back to the I chord. Neighboring motion is when a voice moves stepwise in one direction and then returns to the original pitch by moving stepwise in the opposite direction.

Overlapped Voices

The part-writing weakness of overlapped voices was covered in chapter 7. Further potential exists for this voice leading problem when we use triads in first inversion. An overlapped voice is when a voice moves above a pitch that was just sounded in one of the higher voices in the previous harmony. It can also occur when a voice moves below a pitch that was just sounded in one of the lower voices. Such voice leading confuses the ear and gives the impression that the voices are not maintaining their relative positions, as in crossed voices.

Example 9.6 - Overlapped Voices

The tenor moves up to E, which is higher than the D of the alto in the previous chord.

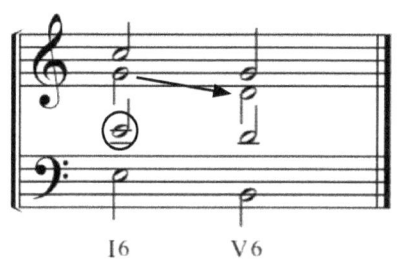

The alto moves down to D, which is lower than the E of the tenor in the previous chord.

Check Your Understanding 9.1

In Ex. 1 below, identify the overlapped voice. Rewrite the example immediately to the right, but re-voice the chords to avoid the overlap.

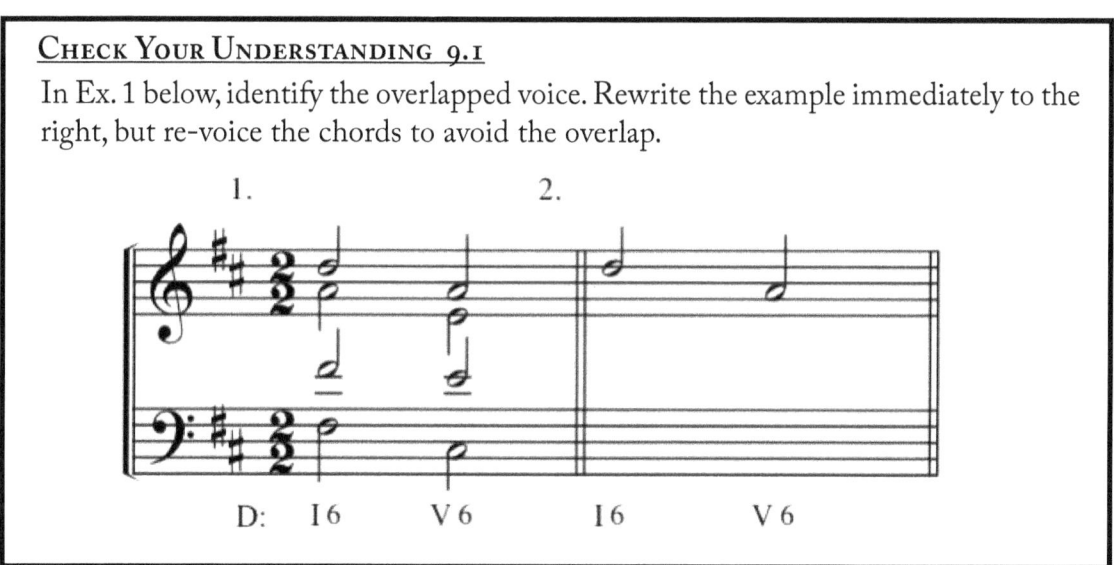

Examples of Doubling in First Inversion Major and Minor Triads

Below is a short excerpt that uses a variety of first inversion triads. Analyze the doubling for each triad.

Example 9.7 - Doubling of 1st Inversion Major and Minor Triads

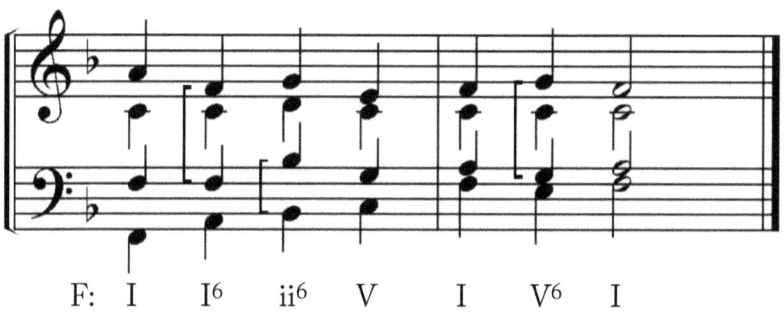

Notice that for the I⁶ in the first measure and the V⁶ in the second measure, the soprano was doubled with an inner voice. This is always the preferred doubling. However, the ii⁶ chord in the first measure has the bass tone doubled with an inner voice. As mentioned earlier, this is also an acceptable doubling, and it was necessary here to avoid a forbidden parallel. If we had doubled the soprano G with a G in the tenor on the ii⁶ chord, there would have been parallel 8ves between the tenor and soprano. When two first inversion chords appear in a row in a four-part texture, you will often have difficulty unless you change the doubling procedure for the second chord.

CHECK YOUR UNDERSTANDING 9.2

Complete these exercises. Double the soprano for first inversion triads if possible, but consider a different doubling if there are more than one first inversion triads in a row.

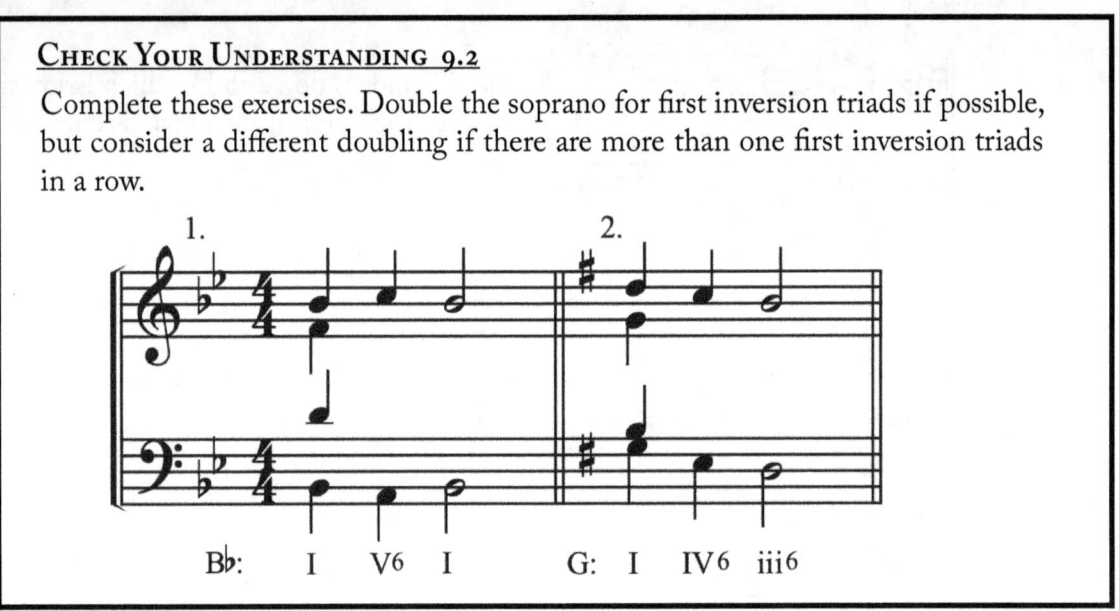

DIMINISHED TRIADS IN FIRST INVERSION: USAGE AND DOUBLING

Here is another short example in the key of F that uses first inversion triads. Examine the vii° chord carefully.

EXAMPLE 9.8 - DOUBLING OF 1ST INVERSION DIMINISHED TRIADS

The vii°⁶ is written in first inversion and the bass tone (3rd of the chord) is doubled. This particular doubling is necessary due to the prominent tritone in this and all diminished triads.

Example 9.9 - Diminished Triad Characteristics

Diminished triads should only be written in first inversion with the 3rd in the bass voice, as was done with this vii°6 chord in example 9.8. Also, make sure to double the chord tone 3rd (double the bass).

Diminished triads have a prominent tritone between the root and 5th.

In all diminished triads, it is necessary to deemphasize the tritone by strengthening the 3rd. This is achieved by placing the third in the bass and doubling it.

Write all diminished triads in first inversion and double the bass.

Check Your Understanding 9.3
Complete these exercises in four parts. Make sure to double the bass for the first inversion diminished triads.

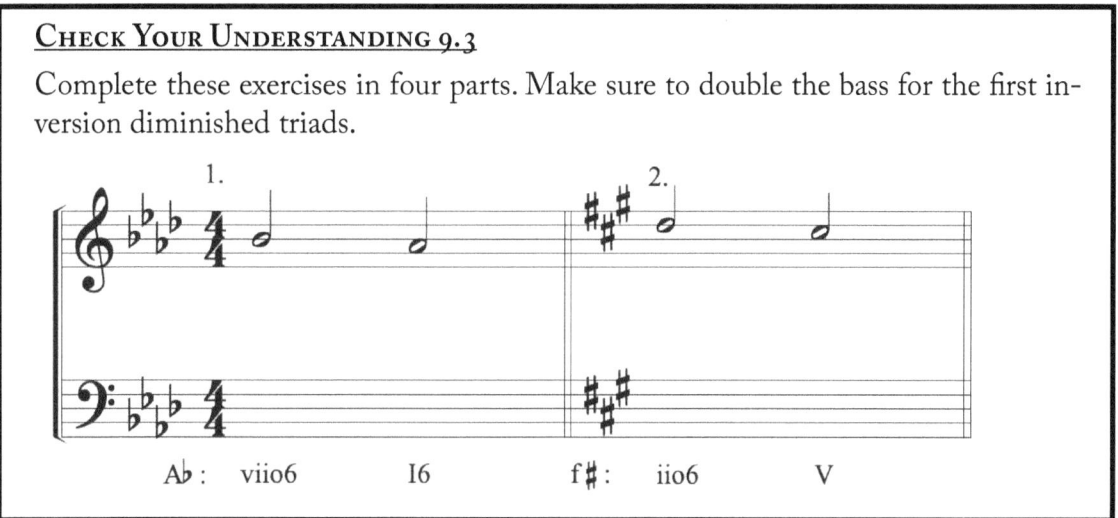

The Phrygian Half Cadence

The Phrygian cadence (iv6 to V) is a special half cadence in a minor key that involves a first inversion iv chord moving to dominant, as shown in example 9.10:

Example 9.10 - The Phrygian Half Cadence

This cadence has a unique sound because the bass moves a half step down (Ab to G) as it resolves into dominant. This half-step motion downward resembles the idiomatic cadence of the ancient Phrygian mode from the 15th century. When voicing the chords, just remember to double the soprano in the iv6 chord and lead stepwise into the leading tone to avoid parallel 5ths.

EXAMPLE 9.11 - THE PHRYGIAN HALF CADENCE IN VOLKSLIEDCHEN (FOLK SONG)

Robert Schumann: *Album for the Young*
No. 9. *Volksliedchen* (Folk Song)
(A longer excerpt of this piece is in Appendix G.)

D: i V⁶ i iv⁶ V
         Phrygian half cadence

CHECK YOUR UNDERSTANDING 9.4

Complete these harmonizations using a Phrygian half cadence. The soprano is given.

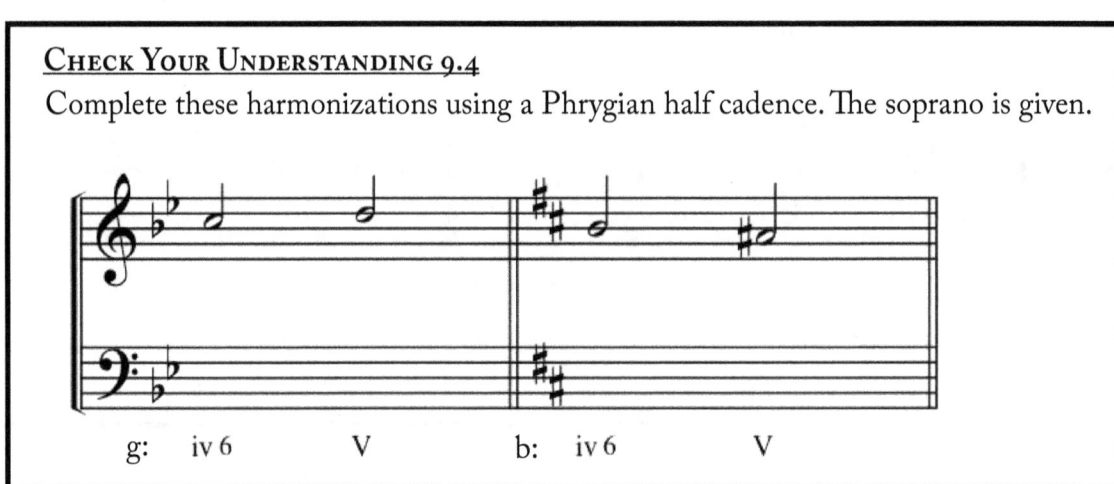

g: iv 6 V   b: iv 6 V

Exercise 9.1

Fill in the missing voices in these short examples.

EXERCISE 9.2

Harmonize in four parts. Use all root position triads unless an inversion is specified. Use secondary triads where indicated by "sec." Do not use any diminished chords. Include a complete Roman numeral analysis and label each cadence.

Exercise 9.3

Harmonize in four parts. Use all root position triads unless an inversion is specified. Use secondary triads only where indicated by the Roman numerals or by the designation "sec." There are diminished chords in these exercises. Include a complete Roman numeral analysis and label each cadence.

Chapter 10: Second Inversion Triads: The Cadential $^6_4$

Terms and Concepts in This Chapter		
second inversion	cadential $^6_4$	doubling for $^6_4$ triads
arpeggiating $^6_4$	cadential $^6_4$ function	rhythmic placement for cadential $^6_4$

Second Inversion Triads

Second inversion triads are written with the 5th of the chord in the bass voice. They are the least stable of all the inversions. Examine the intervals in this voicing for a second inversion C major triad below:

Example 10.1 - C Major Triad in Second Inversion

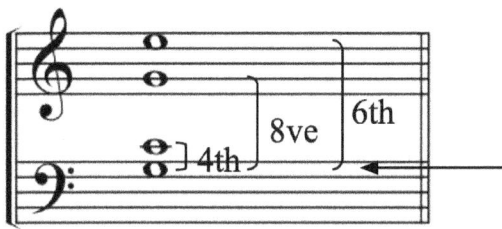

— 5th of the chord is in the bass voice.

In example 10.1, the second inversion triad includes the interval of the 4th between the G in the bass and the C in a higher voice. The interval of the 4th in this position produces a rather unstable sound, and for this reason, the second inversion triad does not project a clear function unless it is closely associated with other harmonies. Here is an example where chord function is determined by a set of chords that include the second inversion triad:

The Arpeggiating $^6_4$ Chord

Example 10.2 - Arpeggiating I $^6_4$

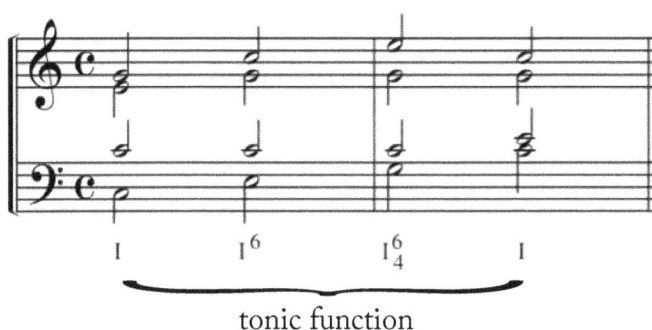

tonic function

Notice that the third chord in this example has the label "$^6_4$" to indicate that it is in second inversion. These numbers refer to the intervals above the bass as shown in example 10.1. The **arpeggiating $^6_4$** is always presented as a series of chords with the same Roman numeral identity, but in a variety of voicings and inversions, often creating an arpeggiating pattern in the bass. Thus, the identification of the tonic function can be made for the entire series of chords. Also note in example 10.2 that the second inversion chord has the **bass pitch doubled**. This is the normal doubling for all $^6_4$ chords.

The Cadential $^6_4$ Chord

Example 10.3 - Cadential $^6_4$ Chord

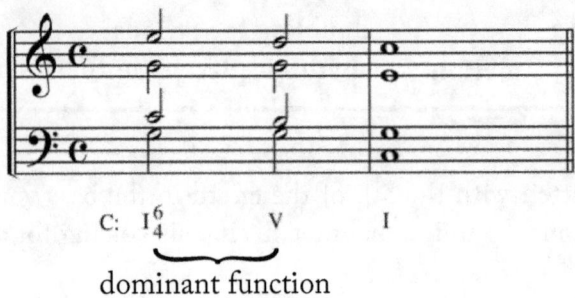

C: I$^6_4$ V   I

dominant function

As its name implies, the **cadential $^6_4$** normally appears at the end of the phrase. The I$^6_4$ chord paired with the following V chord assumes a **dominant function** leading to the final tonic-functioning I chord. Because the I$^6_4$ chord is in a relatively unstable inversion, it gains its strength by introducing the prominent dominant pitch (G) of the key in the bass. The listener hears the arrival of the dominant, but with rather unsettled pitches in the upper voices. The following V chord that contains a repetition of the dominant pitch, again in the bass, further reinforces the sound of dominant function. Here are a few rules that must be followed to produce a satisfactory effect with the cadential $^6_4$:

- The cadential $^6_4$ chord is always **paired with the V chord** to create an area of dominant function.
- The cadential $^6_4$ chord should arrive on a **strong beat**. Otherwise, the perception of dominant function will not be perceived. In $^4_4$ time, it should appear on beat 1 or beat 3, and in $^3_4$ time, it should appear on beat 1 or beat 2.
- The cadential $^6_4$ chord should have a **doubled bass pitch** to further emphasize its dominant function.
- The **bass pitch should remain the same** as the I$^6_4$ moves to V. It is also quite idiomatic if the bass pitch drops an octave when moving from I$^6_4$ to V.
- The upper three voices will contain **one common tone** that should be retained, and **two pitches that should resolve stepwise down** from the I$^6_4$ to the V.

Rhythmic Placement of the Cadential $^6_4$ Chord

Below are short examples that use cadential $^6_4$ chords. In each case, the example to the left has a mistake or weakness. The example to the right is a corrected version.

Example 10.4 - Rhythmic Placement of Cadential $^6_4$ Chord

a. incorrect   b. correct

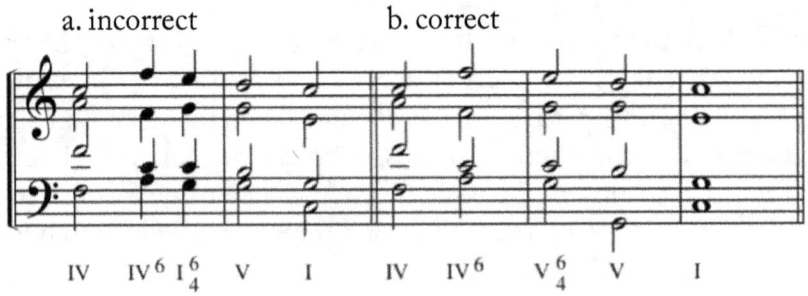

IV   IV^6 I$^6_4$ V   I   IV   IV^6 V$^6_4$ V   I

In example "a" above, the cadential $^6_4$ is on beat 4, the weakest beat of the measure. You should write the I$^6_4$ on a strong beat, either beat 1 or beat 3 in $^4_4$ time, as in example "b" above.

Example 10.5 - Rhythmic Placement of Cadential $^6_4$ Chord

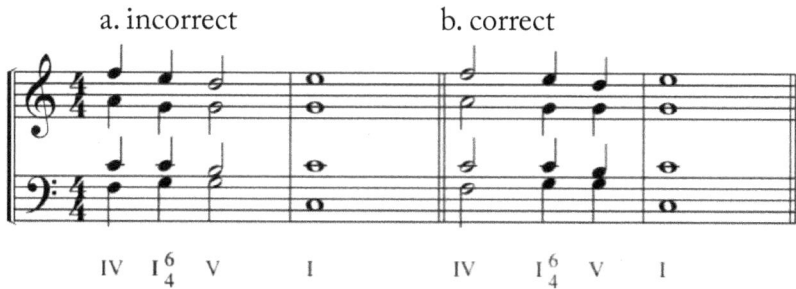

Again, the I$^6_4$ is on a relatively weak beat in example "a." It has been shifted to the stronger beat 3 in example "b."

Example 10.6 - Rhythmic Placement of Cadential $^6_4$ Chord

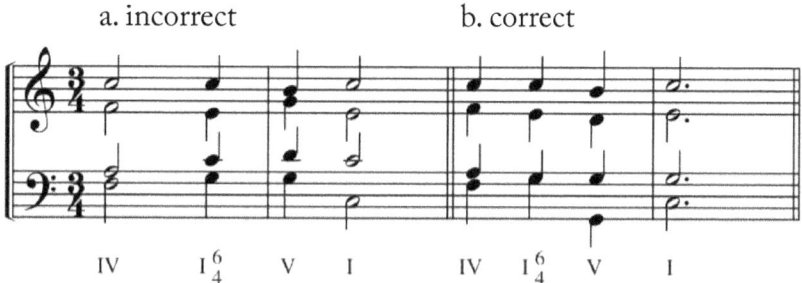

In example "a," there are several mistakes:
- The I$^6_4$ chord should be on a stronger beat than the V chord.
- The doubled pitch of the I$^6_4$ chord should be the bass tone.
- As I$^6_4$ goes to V, the moving pitches should resolve stepwise down.

All of these issues have been fixed in example "b."

Check Your Understanding 10.1

For each example, complete the harmonization in four parts. Use the spacing indicated.

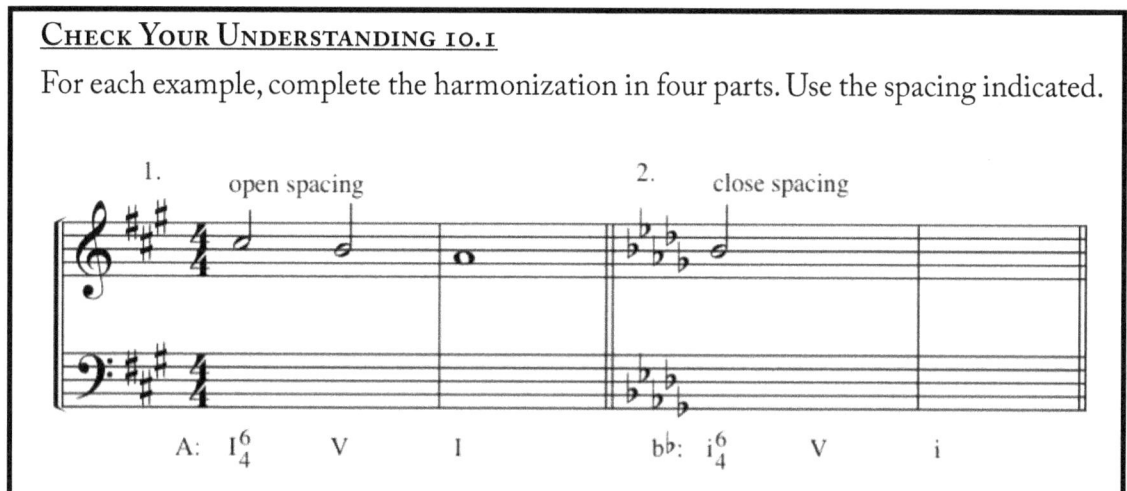

Exercise 10.1

Complete these harmonization examples.

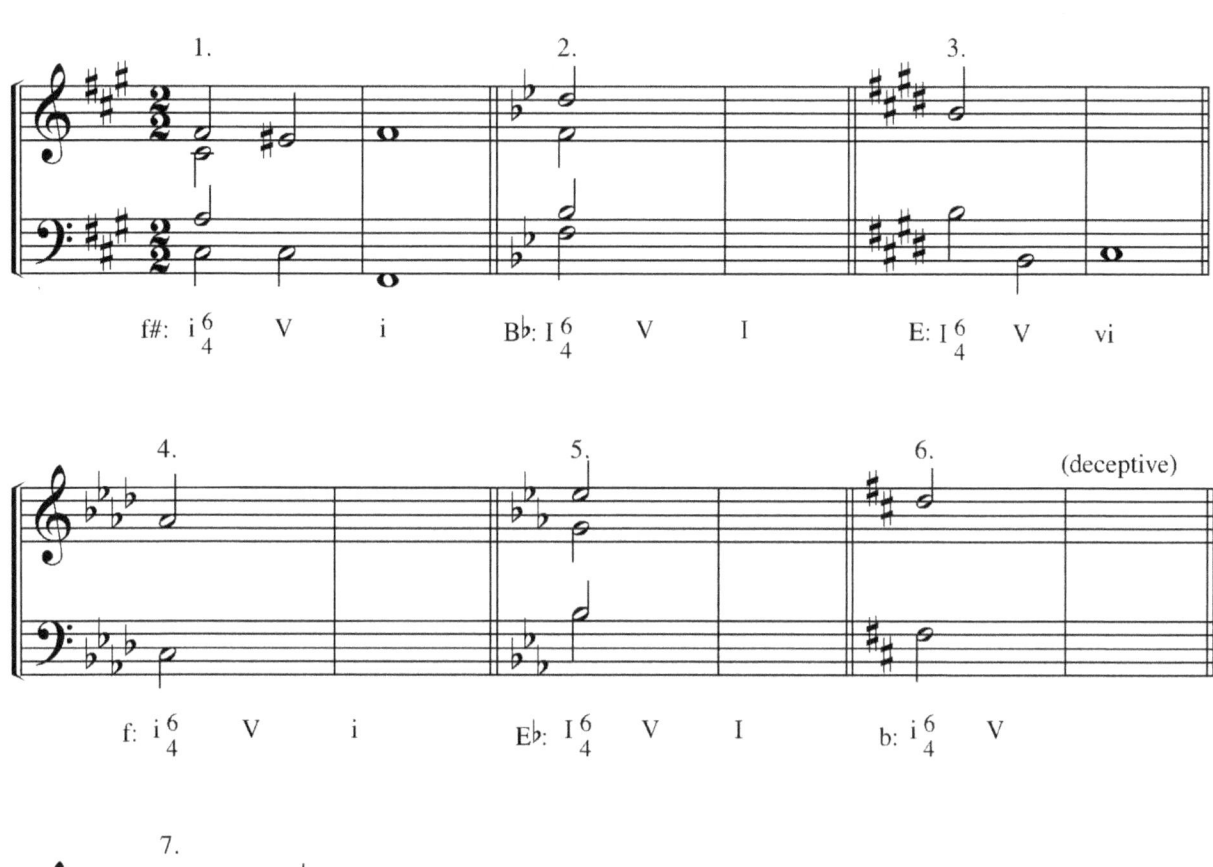

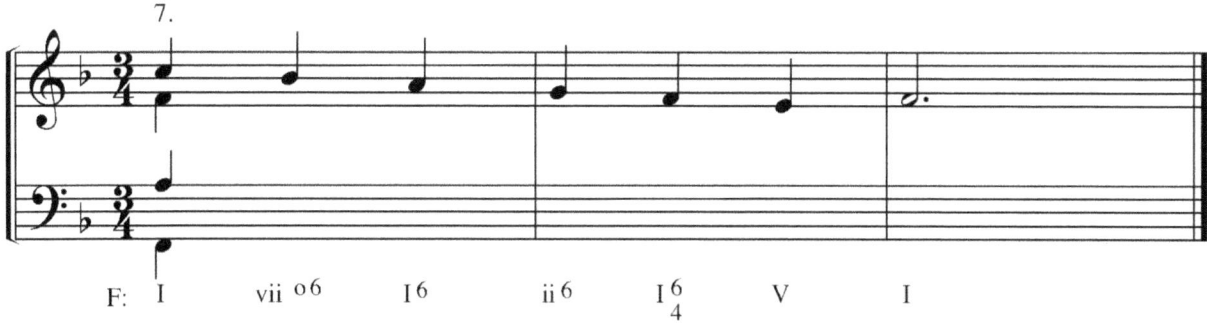

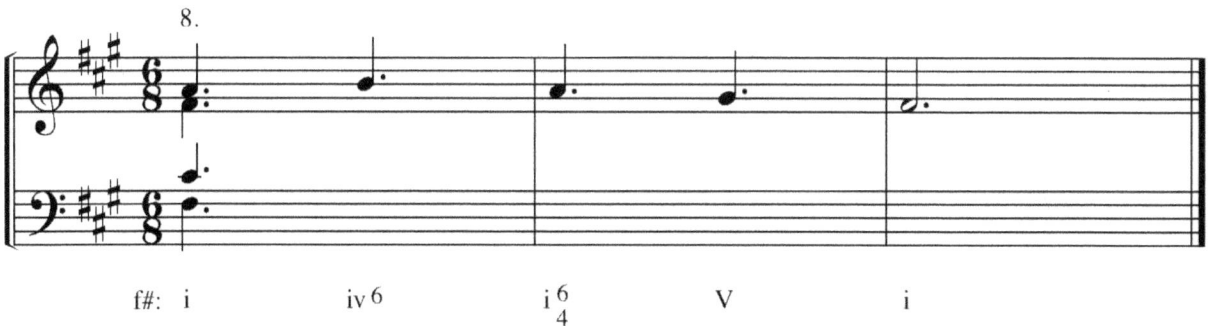

Exercise 10.2

Realize the given harmonizations in four parts.

Exercise 10.3

On the staff below, create your own chorale in four parts by using the following harmonic progression: I viio6 I6 IV ii6 I$^6_4$ V I

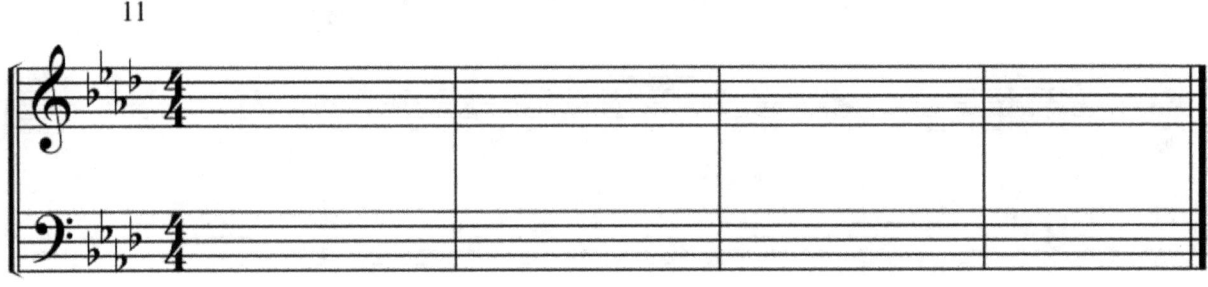

Chapter 11: The Pedal and Passing $^6_4$

> **TERMS AND CONCEPTS IN THIS CHAPTER**
>
> passing $^6_4$ pedal $^6_4$

Special care must be given when writing second inversion triads due to their relative instability. We have already learned that chord function is determined by stronger supporting chords with the arpeggiating $^6_4$ and the cadential $^6_4$. Two other situations in which strong supporting chords help determine the function of second inversion chords are the **passing $^6_4$** progression and the **pedal $^6_4$** progression.

THE PASSING $^6_4$ CHORD

EXAMPLE 11.1 - PASSING I $^6_4$

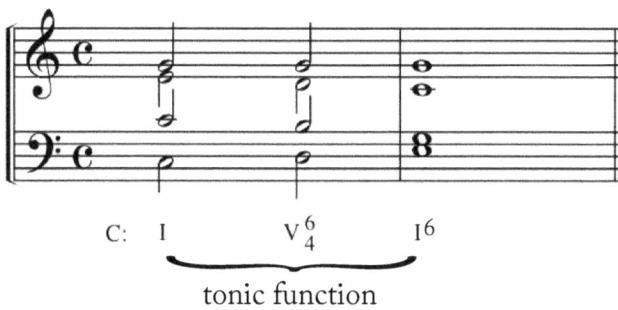

In this progression, the structural harmonies are the tonic triad in root position at the beginning and the tonic triad in first inversion at the end. The V chord in second inversion is somewhat decorative, and seems to be a result of prominent stepwise passing motion in the bass and in the alto. Here are some guidelines to follow when writing a **passing $^6_4$**:

- The passage that contains a passing $^6_4$ chord should **begin with a root position triad and end with the same triad in first inversion.** Between them is a second inversion triad that creates passing motion in the bass.

- Alternately, the progression can **begin with a first inversion triad and end with the same triad in root position.**

- The passing $^6_4$ chord should occur on a **relatively weak beat.**

- The second inversion triad should have a **doubled bass.**

- There is usually **passing motion in one of the upper voices** that is contrary to the **passing motion in the bass.**

- Typically, the structural chords in a passing $^6_4$ progression are either the tonic chord (resulting in tonic function) or the subdominant chord (resulting in dominant preparation function).

Given the guidelines above, there are only four different progressions that typically use the passing $^6_4$ chord, as shown below:

Example 11.2 - Passing $^6_4$ Chord Possibilities

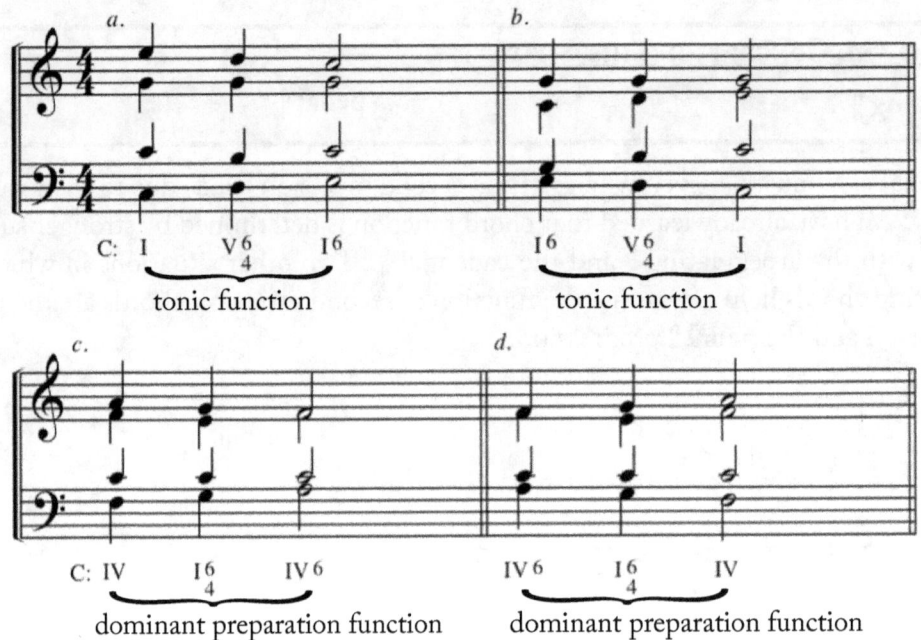

In progressions a. and b. above, the harmonic function is tonic, and in progressions c. and d., the harmonic function is dominant preparation.

Check Your Understanding 11.1
Complete these examples using passing $^6_4$ chords.

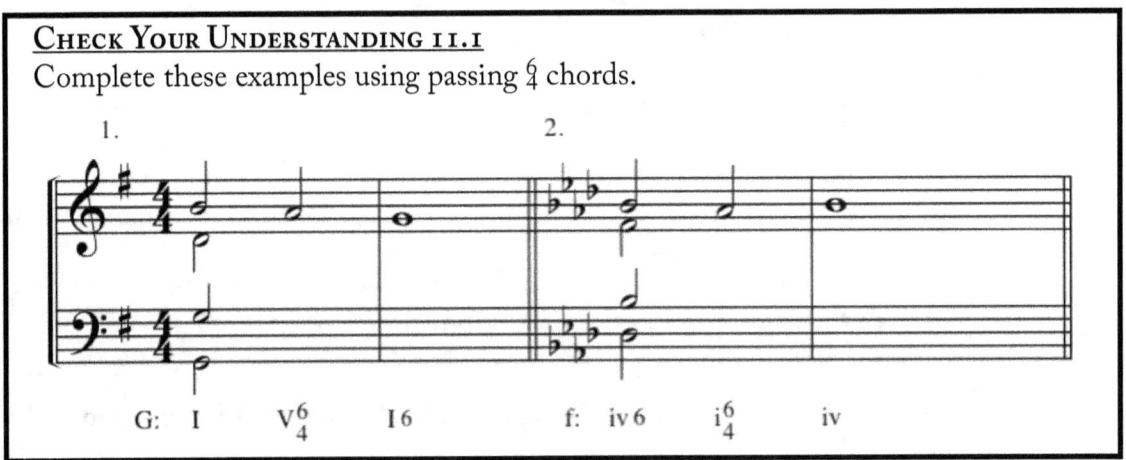

The Pedal $^6_4$ Chord

Example 11.3 - The Pedal $^6_4$ Chord

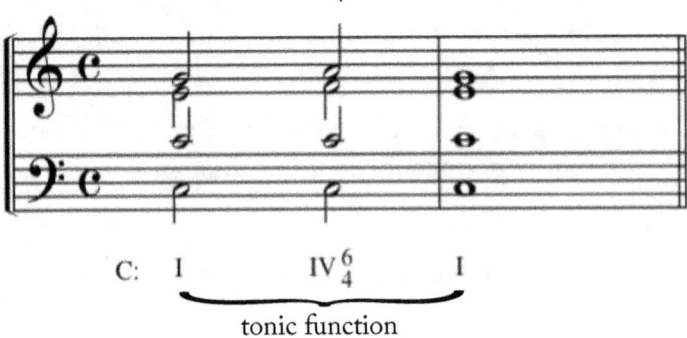

In the **pedal $^6_4$** progression, the first and last chord are the exact same chord in root position. The intervening chord is a second inversion triad that shares the same bass note. The result is called a pedal tone, a pitch in one voice that stays constant even as the chords change. Here are some guidelines to follow when writing a pedal $^6_4$:

- The passage that contains a pedal $^6_4$ chord should **begin with a root position triad and end with the same triad in root position**. Between them is a second inversion triad that creates a pedal tone (the same tone) in the bass.

- The pedal $^6_4$ chord should occur on a **relatively weak beat**.

- The second inversion triad should have a **doubled bass**.

- There is usually **neighboring motion in two of the upper voices** as the progression moves into and then out of the second inversion triad. In fact, the progression is sometimes called a neighboring $^6_4$.

- Typically, the structural chords in a pedal $^6_4$ progression are either the tonic chord (resulting in tonic function) or the dominant chord (resulting in dominant function).

Given the guidelines above, there are only two different progressions that typically use the pedal $^6_4$ chord, as shown below:

Example 11.4 - Pedal $^6_4$ Possibilities

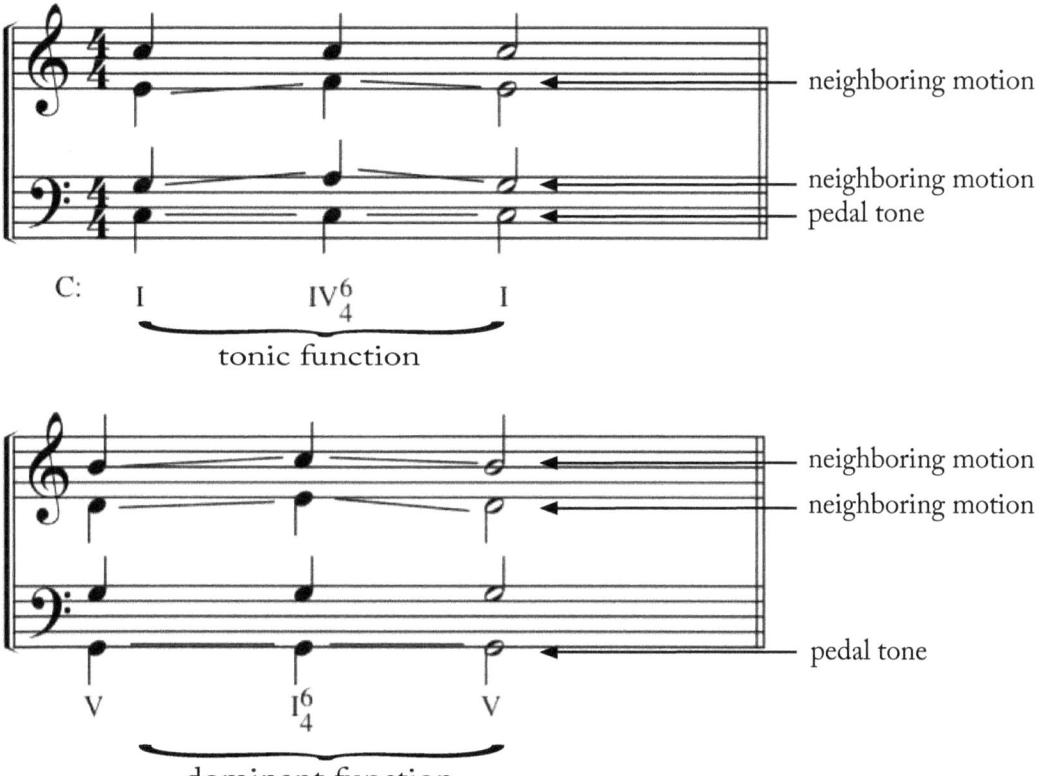

Check Your Understanding 11.2

Complete these examples using a pedal $^6_4$.

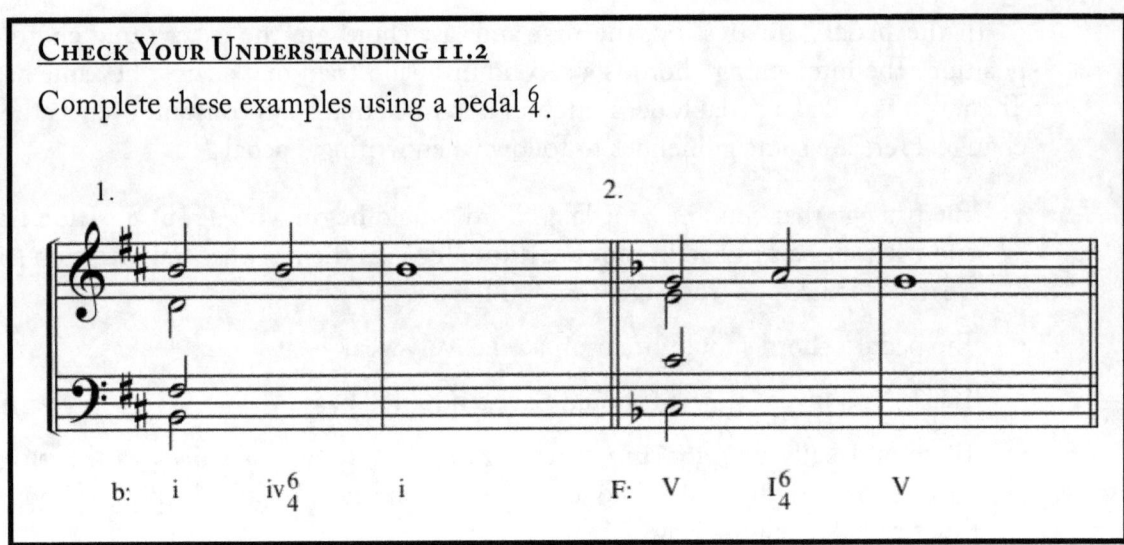

EXERCISE 11.1

Complete the following examples using one of the typical passing $^6_4$ progressions as outlined in example 11.2.

EXERCISE 11.2

Complete the following examples using one of the typical pedal $^6_4$ progressions as outlined in example 11.4.

Exercise 11.3
Realize these figured basses. Note: figured bass is explained in Appendix E.

Exercise 11.4

Complete these harmonizations. Use inversions only where indicated. Use all primary triads unless a secondary triad is indicated by "sec." Label all second inversion chords as "passing," "pedal," or "cadential."

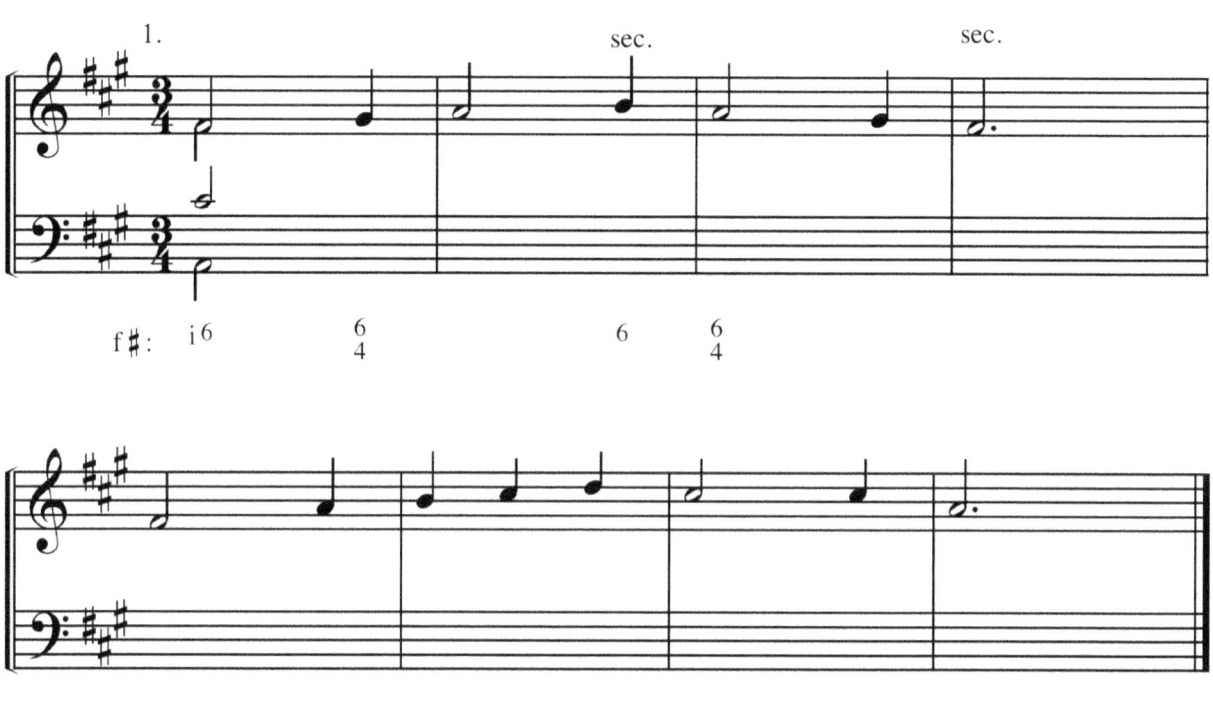

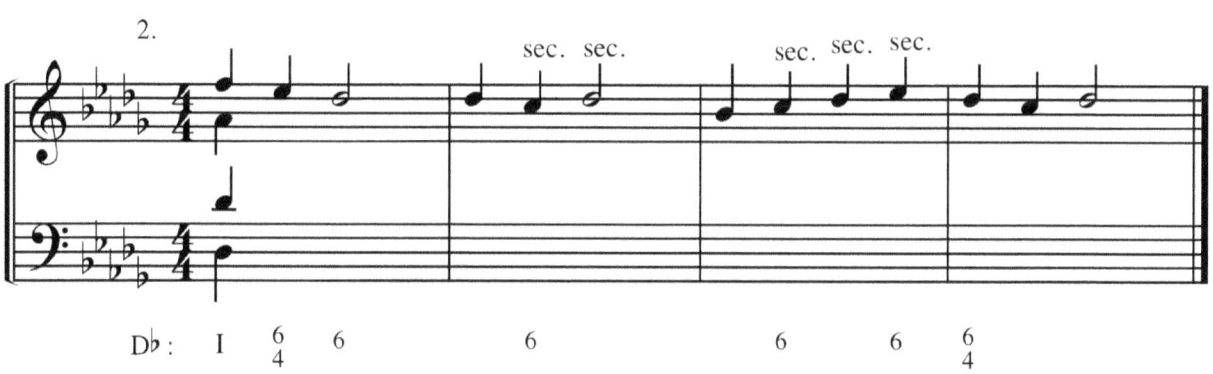

3.

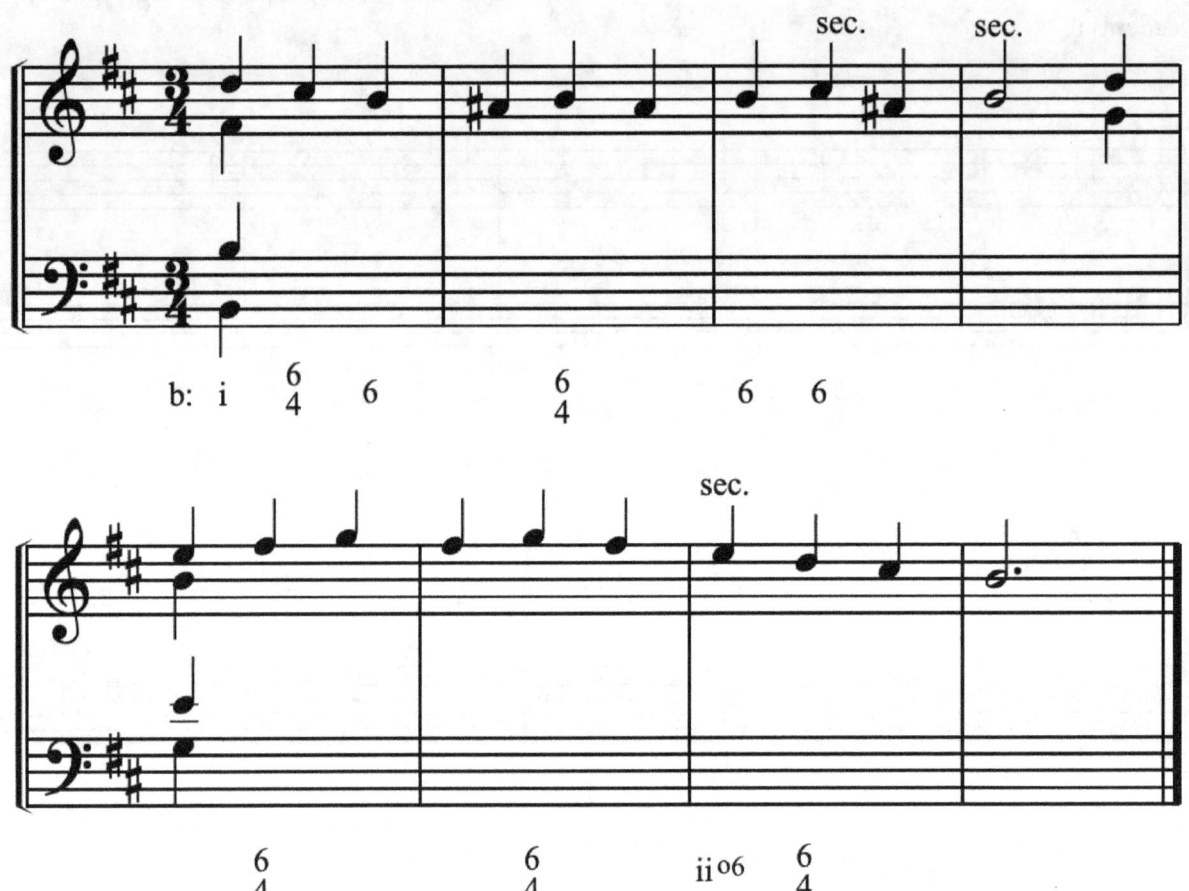

Chapter 12: The Dominant 7th

Terms and Concepts in This Chapter	
seventh chords	leading tone resolution
dominant seventh chord	incomplete chord with omitted 5th
tritone in dominant 7th	strict resolution of leading tone
strict resolution of the chord tone 7th	downward resolution of leading tone

Seventh Chords

Up to this point, we have been working with triads, three-note chords built in thirds. It is also possible to build four-note chords by adding an additional third above the triad. Because this new pitch creates the interval of the 7th above the root tone, we call these chords **seventh chords**. Below are all of the diatonic seventh chords in the key of C:

Example 12.1 - Diatonic Seventh Chords in C Major

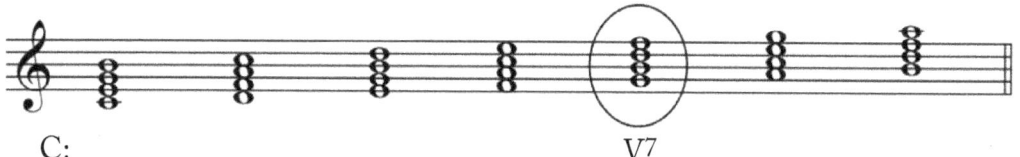

One of the most common seventh chords is the **dominant seventh chord**, built on the 5th scale degree.

Example 12.2 - The Dominant 7 in C Major

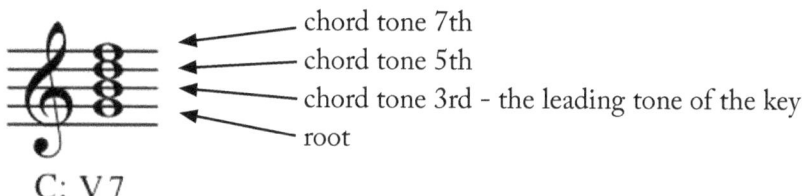

Voice Leading with the Dominant 7 Chord

The dominant 7 chord has a strong **tendency** to progress to the tonic triad, just as the dominant triad does. However, the addition of the chord tone 7th adds extra strength to this progression because it creates a **tritone** interval with the chord tone 3rd (the leading tone).

Example 12.3 - The Tritone in the Dominant 7 Chord

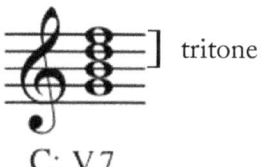

The tritone is a dissonant interval that has a strong tendency to move toward a resolution to a more consonant interval. If we examine the placement of the notes of this interval in the major scale, we see that pitches of the tonic triad are just a half step away, providing a satisfying path to resolution.

Example 12.4 - Resolutions of Tendency Tones in the Dominant 7

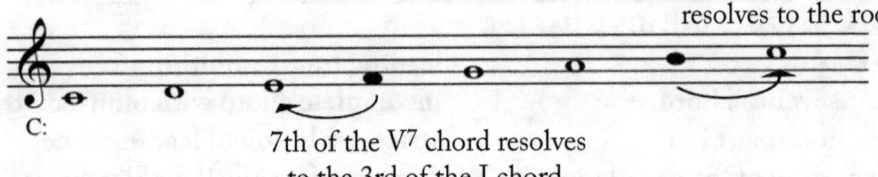

3rd of the V7 chord (the leading tone) resolves to the root of the I chord.

7th of the V7 chord resolves to the 3rd of the I chord.

Here is an example of V7 going to I in four parts that illustrates this voice leading:

Example 12.5 - V7 Resolving to I with 5th Omitted from the I Chord

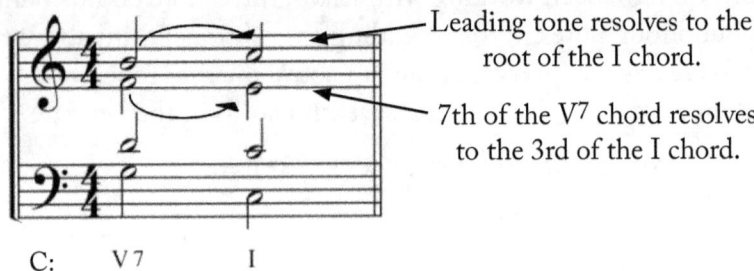

Leading tone resolves to the root of the I chord.

7th of the V7 chord resolves to the 3rd of the I chord.

Notice in example 12.5 that in the V7 chord, each of the voices has a different pitch, and there are no doubled tones. This is possible because 7th chords have four pitches. You should also notice that in the I chord, the **chord tone 5th has been omitted,** and the root tone appears in three different voices. It is not possible to include chord tone 5th in this example because parallel 5ths would occur between the bass and the tenor, as shown below:

Example 12.6 - V7 Resolving to I with Incorrect Parallel 5ths

Incorrect parallel 5ths: a poor solution.

Check Your Understanding 12.1
Resolve these V7 chords into an incomplete tonic triad that contains three root tones and one chord tone 3rd. Make sure to resolve the chord 7th of the V7 chord stepwise down and the leading tone stepwise up.

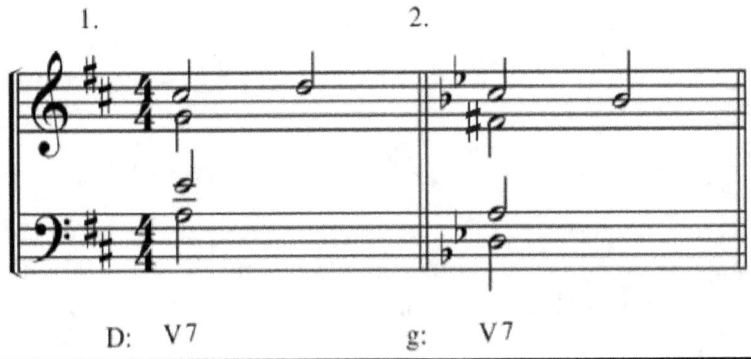

It is important to realize that when resolving a dominant 7 chord, there will always be a compromise in the voice leading between what we may wish to accomplish and what is actually possible to accomplish. This is because we have developed an expectation for the voice leading based upon the procedures we have learned so far. Our natural inclination is to want to resolve the leading tone stepwise up, resolve the chord 7 stepwise down, and write complete chords for both the V7 and the I chord. However, you must always keep in mind that **it is impossible to do all of these things without creating serious voice leading problems**, especially when the V7 chord is in root position. We solve the voice leading dilemma by following one of three possible procedures:

- Omit the 5th of the I chord (this was demonstrated in Example 12.5), or
- Omit the 5th of the V7 chord, or
- Use a downward resolution of the leading tone (this is only an option if the leading tone is in an inner voice).

We have already seen an example of good voice leading from V7 to I in example 12.5 that involved omitting the 5th of the I chord. Below is another good voice leading solution where the 5th has been omitted from the V7 chord.

Example 12.7 - V7 Resolving to I with 5th Omitted from the V7 Chord

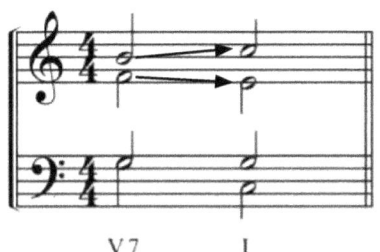

Leading tone resolves up to the root of the I chord.

7th of the V7 chord resolves down to the 3rd of the I chord.

5th of the V7 omitted to avoid parallel 5ths.

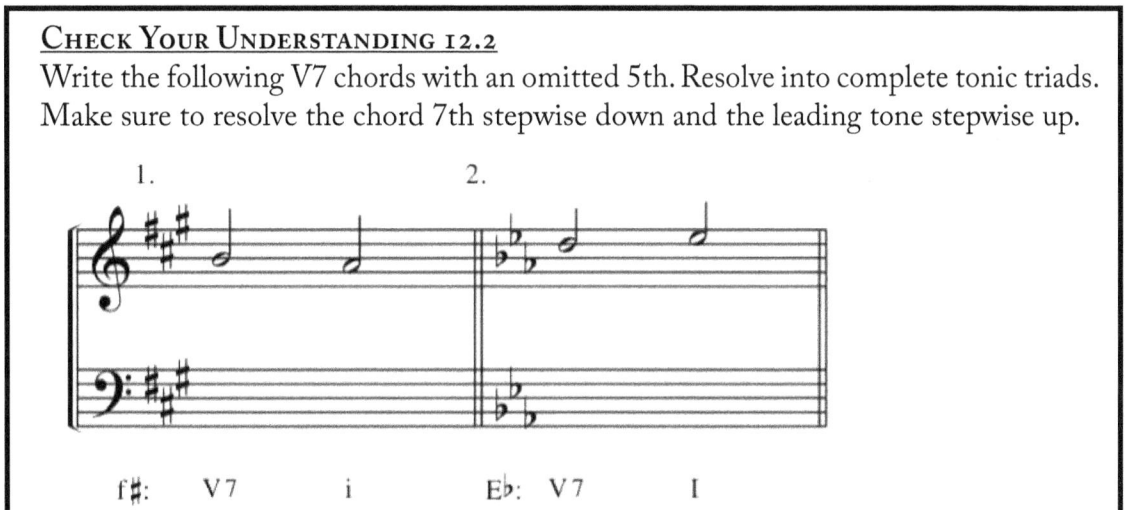

Check Your Understanding 12.2
Write the following V7 chords with an omitted 5th. Resolve into complete tonic triads. Make sure to resolve the chord 7th stepwise down and the leading tone stepwise up.

Downward Resolution of the Leading Tone in an Inner Voice

It is sometimes possible to go against the natural tendency of the leading tone and allow it to resolve downward, as shown in example 12.8.

Example 12.8 - V7 Resolving to I with Downward Resolution of Leading Tone

7th of the V7 chord resolves down to the 3rd of the I chord.

Leading tone resolves downward to the 5th of the I chord.

Both chords are complete (they both include the 5th).

In this solution, both the V7 chord and the I chord are complete; they contain all of their respective chord tones including the 5th. However, the leading tone of the V7 chord did not resolve up to the tonic pitch of the I chord as it did in the previous examples. Here, it **resolved downward by the interval of a third to the 5th of the I chord. This is only acceptable if the leading tone is in an inner voice (alto or tenor).** When it is in an outer voice (bass or soprano), its natural tendency to resolve stepwise up is too strong to ignore. The most common reason for allowing a leading tone to resolve downward is to allow for complete chords on both the V7 and the I.

Check Your Understanding 12.3

For each example, write a complete V7 chord, and then resolve it to a complete tonic triad. Resolve the chord 7th stepwise down, but you will have to resolve the leading tone downward by the interval of a third so that it arrives on the 5th of the I chord.

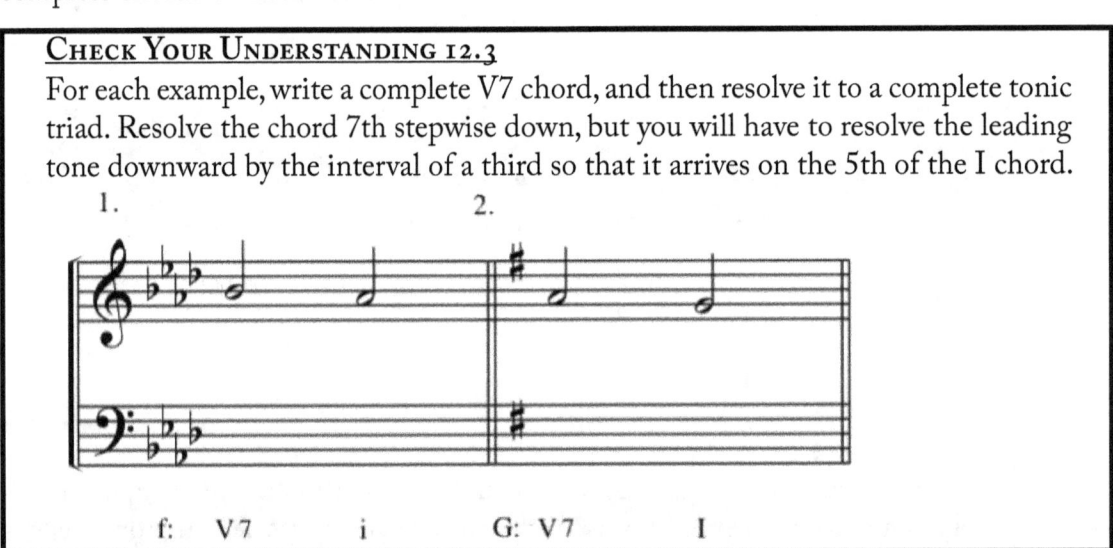

Here is a set of guidelines for resolving dominant 7 chords:

- The **chord tone 7th** of the V7 chord **should always resolve stepwise down**. This is called **the strict resolution of the chord tone 7th,** and this rule is rarely, if ever, broken.
- The **leading tone** in the V7 chord (the chord tone 3rd) **should usually resolve stepwise up**, and this is mandatory if it is in an outer voice (soprano or bass). This is called a **strict resolution** of the leading tone.
- **When using strict resolutions of the leading tone and the chord tone 7th, you must write an incomplete chord for either the V7 chord or the I chord.** On the V7 chord, this is done by omitting the chord tone 5th and doubling the root. If you omit the 5th of the I chord, you should triple the root tone in most cases.
- **If you wish to write a complete chord for both the V7 chord and the I chord, you must resolve the leading tone downward by the interval of a third** so that it arrives on the 5th of the I chord. This is only possible if the leading tone is in an inner voice (alto or tenor).

Exercise 12.1

For each example, determine the key (some are major and some are minor). Then, resolve each dominant 7 chord to a tonic triad. **Use strict resolution of the chord tone 7 (stepwise downward) and strict resolution of the leading tone (stepwise upward).** Determine if the given V7 chord is complete. **If it is complete, you will need to omit the 5th from the I chord and triple the root. If it is incomplete, you should resolve to a complete I chord.** The first example is completed for you.

Exercise 12.2

Resolve each dominant 7 chord to a tonic triad. Use a complete tonic triad in each case. It will be necessary to resolve the leading tone downward by the interval of the third so that it arrives on the 5th of the I chord. The first example has been completed for you.

Exercise 12.3

Complete each of these short progressions. There may be a variety of solutions, so you should decide how to resolve the leading tone and whether to use complete or incomplete chords. The 7th of the V7 should always resolve strictly (stepwise down)

Exercise 12.4

Harmonize this melody in four parts. Use inversions only where indicated. Use dominant 7th chords only where indicated. Use secondary triads only where indicated by "sec." Provide a Roman numeral analysis underneath. Add at least one passing tone, one neighbor tone, and 1 suspension. Note: non-chord tones such as passing tones, neighbor tones, and suspensions are explained in appendices C and D.

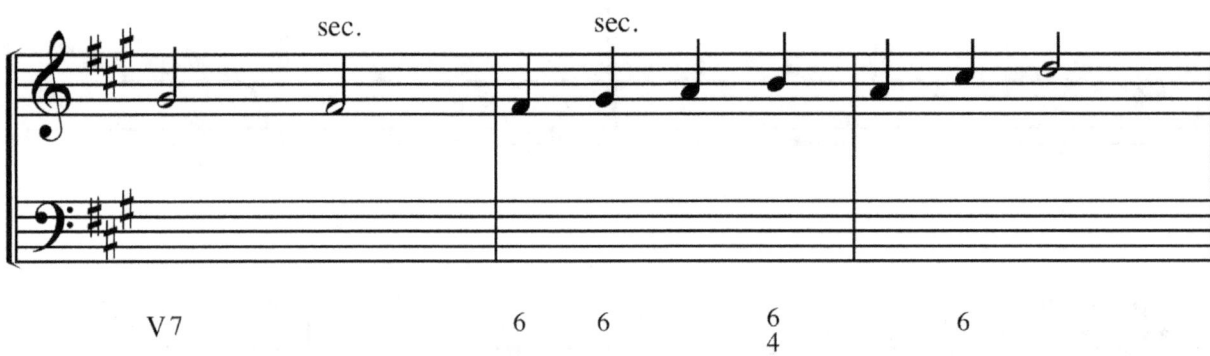

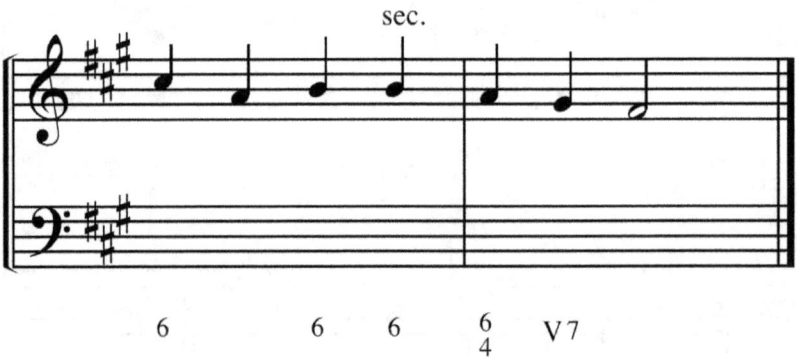

Exercise 12.5

Complete these figured basses. You may add additional non-chord tones. Provide a Roman numeral analysis underneath. Note: figured bass is explained in appendix E and non-chord tones are explained in appendices C and D.

1.

2.

100

Chapter 13: Inversions of Dominant 7th

> **TERMS AND CONCEPTS IN THIS CHAPTER**
> 7: root position 7th chord $^4_3$: first inversion 7th chord
> $^6_5$: first inversion 7th chord   2: first inversion 7th chord

INVERSIONS OF THE SEVENTH CHORD

As with triads, it is possible to invert seventh chords by placing a chord tone in the bass that is other than the tonic. The root position version of the dominant 7 chord in the key of C along with its three possible inversions are written below with all the intervals above the bass pitch labeled. The Roman numeral with figured bass designation is written below each. Notice that the figured bass designation is an abbreviated version of the intervals above the bass.

EXAMPLE 13.1 - SEVENTH CHORD IN ROOT POSITION AND IN INVERSIONS

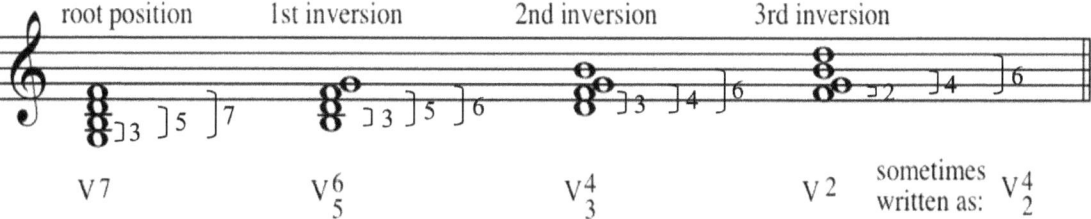

Remember that when voicing chords, the **inversion is determined solely by the pitch that is in the bass**, regardless of where the other chord tones are located. You can use the chart below to help you when determining the specific inversions for seventh chords.

EXAMPLE 13.2 - CHART OF FIGURED BASS SYMBOLS FOR 7TH CHORDS

Chord Tone in the Bass	Root Position or Inversion	Figured Bass Symbol
Root	root position	7
3rd	1st inversion	$^6_5$
5th	2nd inversion	$^4_3$
7th	3rd inversion	2

When resolving inverted dominant seventh chords in four voices, there is seldom the need to write incomplete chords or to resolve the leading tone freely as with root position dominant seven chords. In most cases it is possible to write complete chords for both the dominant seventh and the tonic and to also resolve the leading tone stepwise up and the chord seventh stepwise down. However, it may be necessary to resolve into an inversion of the tonic triad when leading from an inverted dominant seventh. Below are some examples:

Example 13.3 - Resolution of Inverted V7 Chords

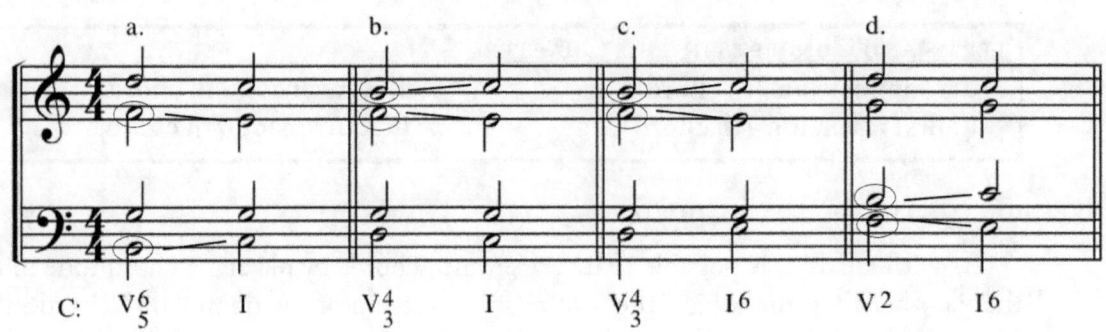

Note that in each example presented above, the leading tone resolved strictly (stepwise up), the chord tone 7th resolved strictly (stepwise down), and all the chords were complete.

It is important to note that some inversions of the dominant seventh chord necessitate resolution to specific inversions of the I chord. In example a. above, the 1st inversion dominant seventh chord has the leading tone in the bass, and, being an outer voice, it must resolve upward into the root of the I chord. In example d., the chord seventh is in the bass, and this time, as an outer voice, it must resolve downward to the third of the I chord.

Check Your Understanding 13.1
Write the following inverted dominant 7th chords in four voices and resolve them to tonic. Use all complete chords. Use strict resolutions of the leading tone and chord tone 7th.

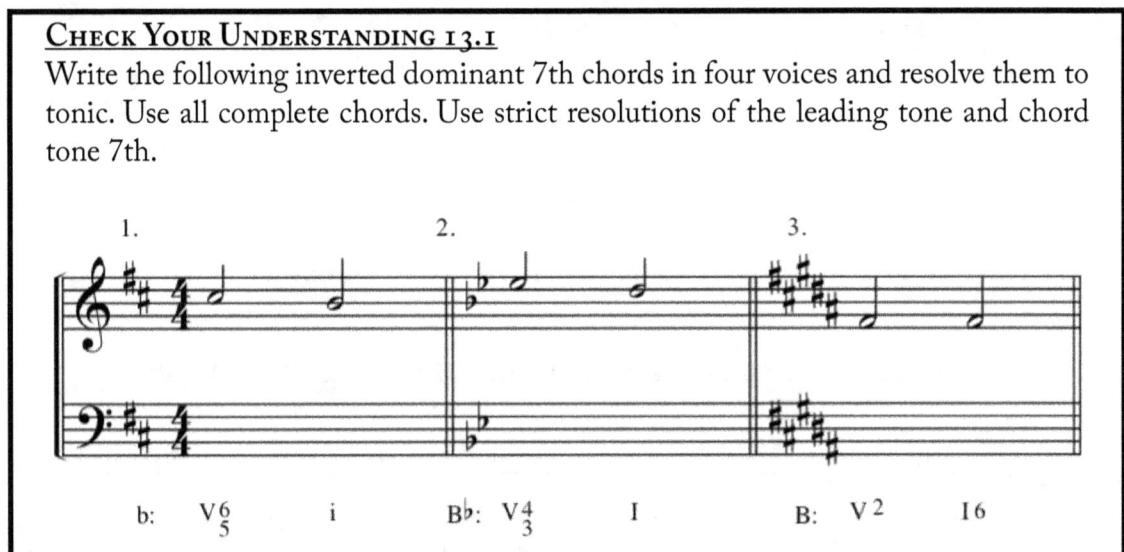

Exercise 13.1

Complete these short examples in four parts by resolving the given dominant seven chord into a tonic chord in either root position or an appropriate inversion if necessary. Resolve the chord 7th strictly (stepwise down) and the leading tone strictly (stepwise up).

Exercise 13.2
Realize these figured basses. Feel free to add additional non-chord tones

Chapter 14: Other Diatonic Seventh Chords

> TERMS AND CONCEPTS IN THIS CHAPTER
> major-minor 7 chord
> major-major 7 chord
> minor-minor 7 chord
> diminished-minor 7 chord
> half diminished 7 chord
> diminished-diminished 7 chord
> fully diminished 7 chord

QUALITIES OF SEVENTH CHORDS

The last two chapters have focused on the dominant seventh chord, but keep in mind that any diatonic chord can be built up to the seventh. To further explore these structures, it is necessary to catalogue all of the common sonorities of seventh chords. The easiest way to assimilate these qualities is by labeling the quality of the triad in conjunction with the quality of the seventh. For example, the dominant seventh chord that we have already discussed has a major quality triad, and this is paired with a minor 7th interval between the root and the seventh. Because of these features, we identify the quality of the dominant 7th chord as "**major-minor 7th**," abbreviated as **Mm7**.

EXAMPLE 14.1 - THE MAJOR-MINOR 7 QUALITY OF THE DOMINANT 7 CHORD

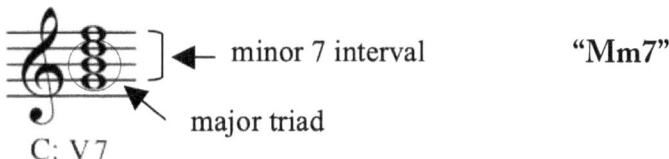

Below is a chart of the most common 7th chord qualities:

EXAMPLE 14.2 - COMMON QUALITIES OF 7TH CHORDS

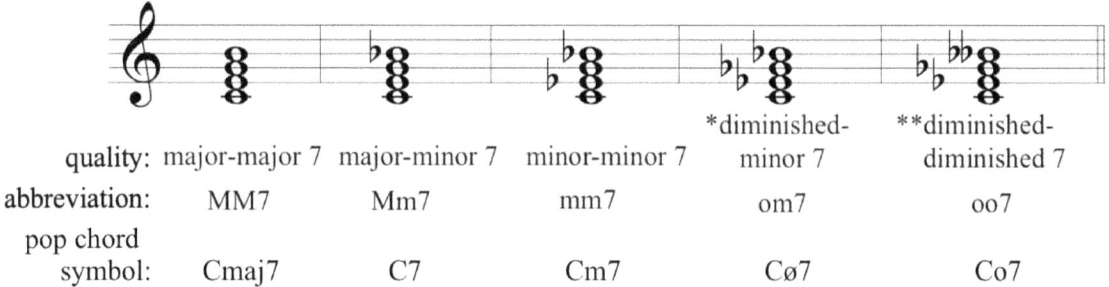

*The **diminished–minor 7** chord is commonly called "**half diminished**." The symbol "ø7" is used to denote this chord quality in traditional Roman numeral analysis as well as with pop chord symbols.

The **diminished–diminished 7 chord is commonly called "**fully diminished**." The symbol "o7" is used to denote this chord quality in traditional Roman numeral analysis as well as with pop chord symbols.

The following two charts show the diatonic 7th chord qualities in a major key and in a minor key:

Example 14.3 - The Diatonic Seventh Chords in C Major

quality:	MM7	mm7	mm7	MM7	Mm7	mm7	øm7
Roman numeral:	I7	ii7	iii7	IV7	V7	vi7	viiø7
pop chord symbol:	Cmaj7	Dm7	Em7	Fmaj7	G7	Am7	Bø7

Example 14.3 - The Diatonic Seventh Chords in C Minor

quality:	mm7	øm7	MM7	mm7	Mm7	MM7	oo7
Roman numeral:	i7	iiø7	III7	iv7	V7	VI7	vii°7
pop chord symbol:	Cm7	Dø7	E♭maj7	Fm7	G7	A♭maj7	B°7

Here are a few things to keep in mind when writing diatonic 7th chords:

- Each chord **can be used in any of its inversions**. The second inversion is most commonly used as a passing or pedal chord, just as discussed with triads in Chapter 12.
- The seventh of the chord should always resolve **stepwise down** unless there is a very compelling melodic reason not to resolve this way.
- If the chord has a leading tone (as in the dominant or leading tone chord), be sensitive to its resolution. **In outer voices, leading tones must resolve stepwise up.**
- Unlike diminished triads, the **diminished and half-diminished 7th chords can be written in root position**.
- The I chord built to the 7th is somewhat unusual until music of the late 19th century.

The ii7 and iiø7 Chords

The ii7 and iiø7 are quite common, especially in root position and first inversion. As dominant preparation chords, they usually lead directly to dominant. Here are some examples:

Example 14.5 - Voice Leading with ii7 and iiø7

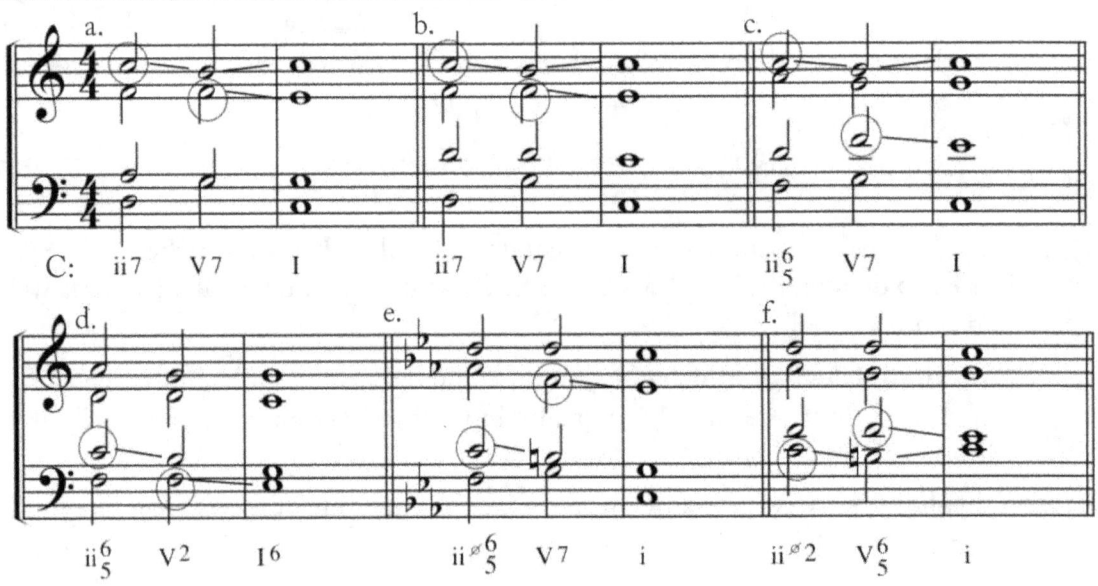

While example 14.5 is not intended to be an exhaustive catalogue of usage, it does illustrate some interesting possibilities. In all cases, the chord sevenths resolve downward, and this is indicated by a circled tone. In addition, the leading tones must resolve stepwise up, but only if in an outer voice. If the leading tone is in an inner voice, it can either resolve stepwise up or it can drop down a 3rd into the chord tone 5th of the following chord (examples d. and c.). Also notice that incomplete chords can be used for the ii7 chords (example b.), the V7 chords (example a. and c.), or the I chords (example b.) in order to facilitate the voice leading.

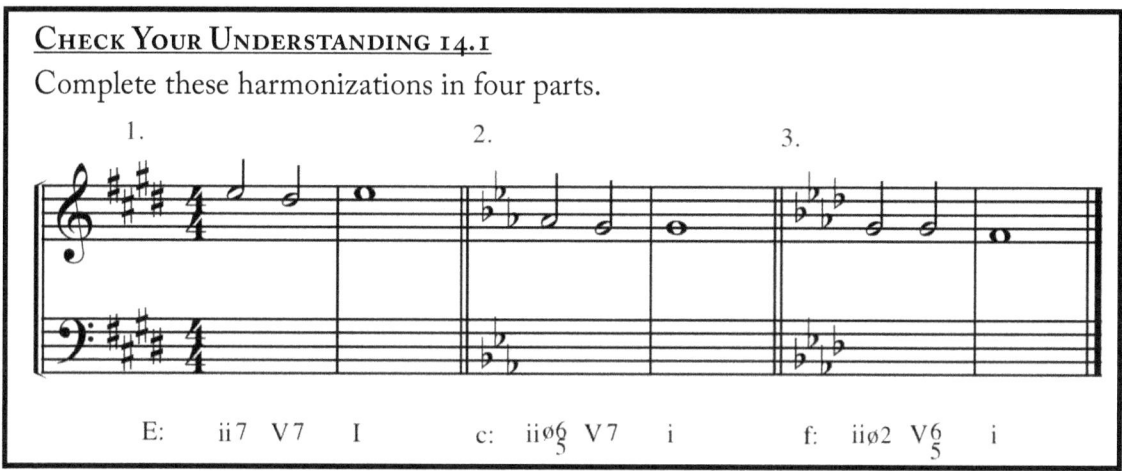

The viiø7 and viio7 Chords

The viiø7 and viio7 are dominant functioning chords that are also commonly used seventh chords. Like the V7, they contain both a leading tone and a chord tone 7th. Unlike the V7, it is possible in the root position viiø7 and viio7 chords to resolve both the leading tone and the chord tone 7th strictly without using incomplete chords. In a major key, the diatonic leading tone chord is viiø7 (half diminished). Some examples are below:

Example 14.6 - Voice Leading with viiø7 in the Key of C Major

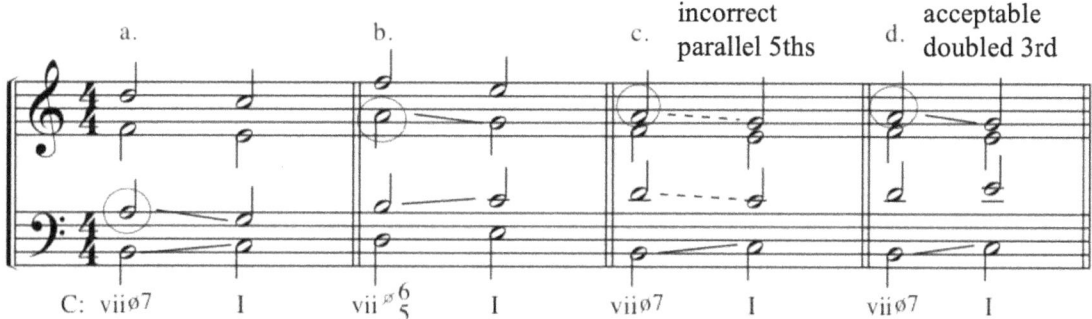

Notice that in each case, the leading tone and the chord tone 7th have been resolved strictly. However, example c. presents one of the fundamental difficulties with progressions using the viiø7 chord: the strong possibility of writing parallel 5ths. In example c., the parallel 5ths appear between the soprano and tenor voices. The reason for this voice leading difficulty is that there is a perfect 5th interval between the chord tone 3rd and the chord tone 7th of the viiø7 chord, and if we are not careful, we may lead this interval to the perfect fifth that exists between the root and the chord tone 5th of the I chord.

Examples a. and b. of example 14.6 did not present the problem of parallel 5ths because the chord tone 7th of the viiø7 chord (A in the tenor) was voiced below the chord tone 3rd (D in the soprano). The parallel 4ths that result are not a voice leading error. When the chord tone 7th of the viiø7 chord is voiced above the chord tone 3rd, the correct solution is to double the 3rd of the I chord, as in example d. This potential issue is only present when using a viiø7 in a major key. When using the leading tone 7th chord in a minor key, the quality is fully diminished (viio7), and there is a tritone interval between the chord tone 3rd and the chord tone 7th. Therefore, there is no possibility of writing parallel 5ths. Some examples are given below:

Example 14.7 - Voice Leading with viio7 in the Key of C Minor

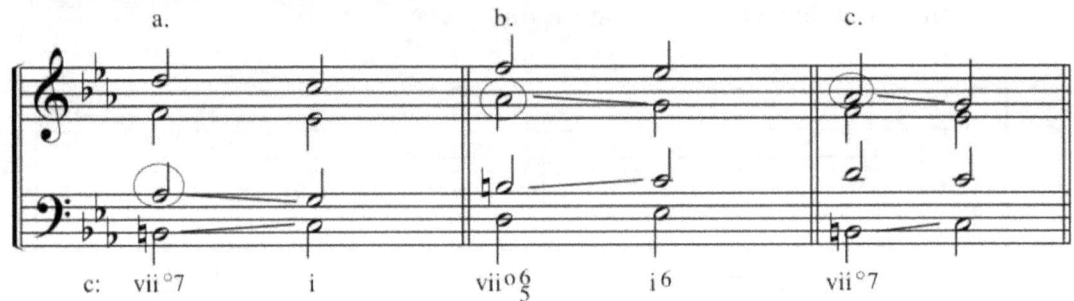

Often, composers will use the fully diminished quality for the leading tone 7th chord even when in a major key. This does require a chromatic alteration, as the fully diminished quality does not fit exactly in the major key. Nevertheless, composers are fond of this progression due to the smooth voice leading and strong, pleasing sound of the fully diminished chord. Here is an example:

Example 14.8 - Voice Leading with viio7 in a Major Key

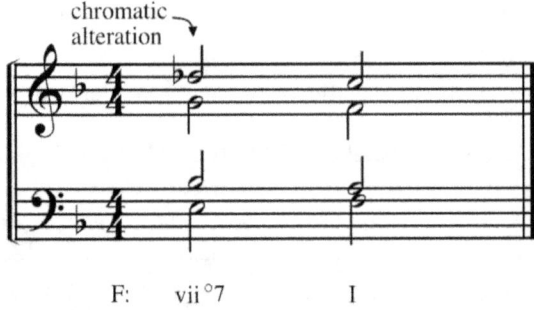

Check Your Understanding 14.2
Harmonize in four parts. Make sure to avoid parallel 5ths in the first two examples.

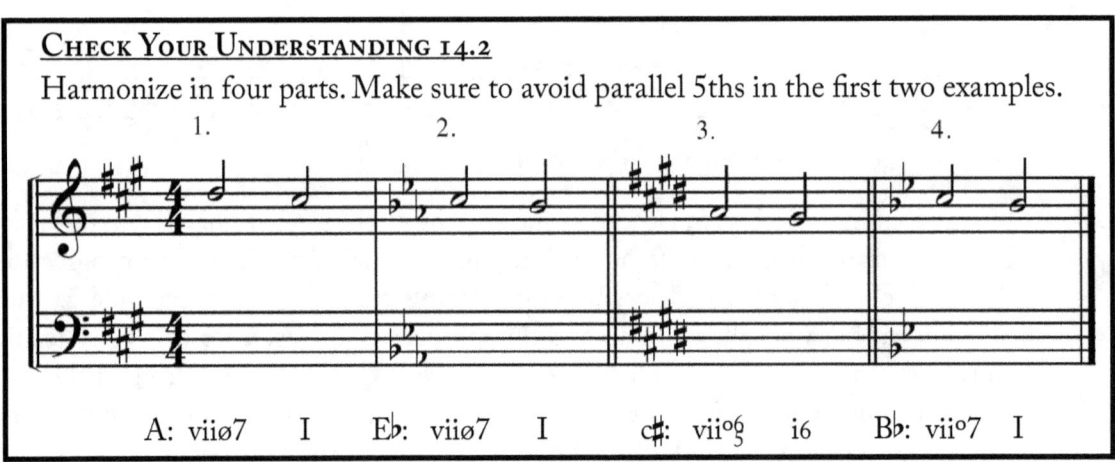

Exercise 14.1

Complete these short progressions in four voices.

Exercise 14.2

Complete these short progressions in four voices. Play close attention to the quality of the leading tone 7th chord, as the fully diminished chord is sometimes used in a major key.

Exercise 14.3

Harmonize in four parts. Use inversions only where indicated. Add at least two suspensions, two passing tones, and two neighbor notes.

Chapter 15: Seventh Chord Sequence in 5ths

> **TERMS AND CONCEPTS IN THIS CHAPTER**
> sequence   authentic sequence
> root tone motion in 5ths   subtonic

THE AUTHENTIC HARMONIC SEQUENCE

A **sequence** is a recurring musical pattern that is manifest in a harmonic progression as well as a melodic phrase. Specifically, the pattern repeats at successively higher or successively lower pitch levels. A common harmonic sequence is a diatonic pattern in which the root tones of the chords drop by the interval of the fifth, and this is called an **authentic sequence**. Such a harmonic series offers a rich opportunity for the introduction of 7ths either as passing tones or as chord tones. The root tones of the chord progression are easy to find by following the path of a descending circle of fifths. Simply start on the key tone (C in this case) and trace the pitches clockwise, skipping over all the pitches that do not fit in the key.

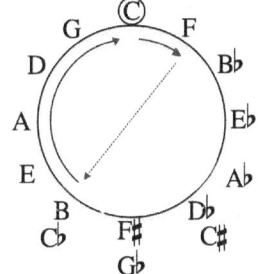

EXAMPLE 15.1 - THE AUTHENTIC SEQUENCE WITH PASSING TONES

a.

C: I 8 - 7   IV 8 - 7   viiø 8-7   iii 8 - 7   vi 8 - 7   ii 8 - 7   V 8 - 7   I

b.

C: I7   IV7   viiø7   iii7   vi7   ii7   V7   I

In example a. of 15.1, the chord tone 7ths are introduced as passing tones while in example b., they are "frozen" in place to produce the seventh-chord sonority on the strong beats of the measures. In each example, the melodic pattern is established in the first measure for all voices, and then the pattern continues in subsequent measures on successively lower pitch levels. Notice that the voice leading for a series of root position 7th chords results in instances where the 5th is omitted on every other chord.

Example 15.2 - The Authentic Sequence using Inversions

In example a. of 15.2, the 7th is introduced as a passing tone in the bass. The result is a series of inverted 7th chords, as is seen more clearly in example b. when the passing tones are frozen in place as chord tones. Once again, the pattern established in the first measure repeats on successively lower pitch levels right to the end of the phrase.

Example 15.3 - The Authentic Sequence in C Minor

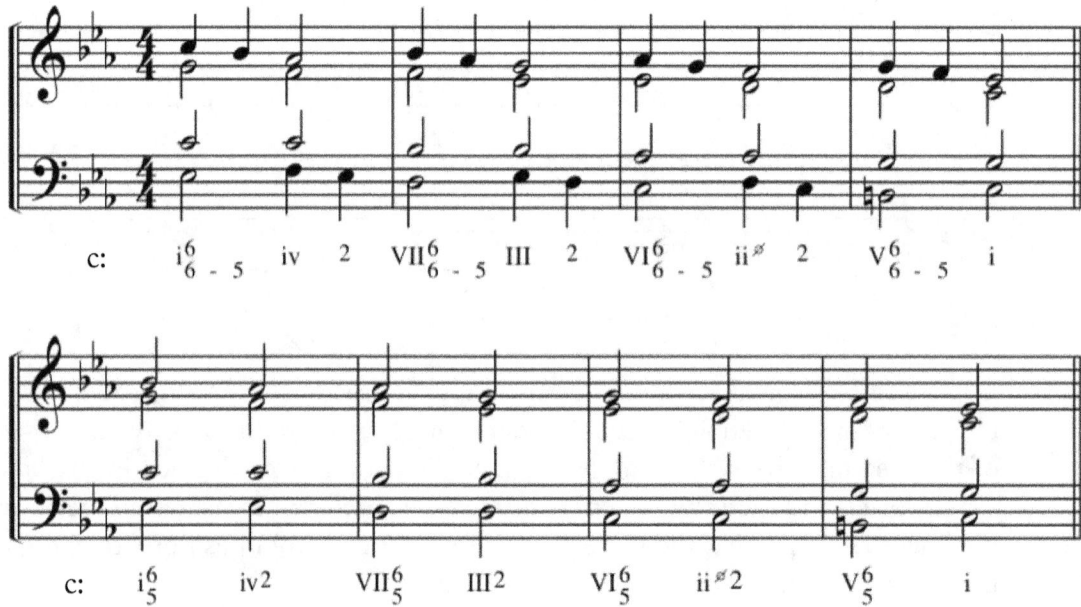

Example 15.3 shows an interesting sequence using a variety of inversions in a minor key. Notice that the leading tone chord is not used in the second measure. Rather, the **subtonic** VII chord is used since the progression is moving to a III chord instead of back to i. The leading tone pitch is not introduced until the penultimate V chord, which finally does lead back to i. This is the most common chord progression for a minor sequence with root tones moving down in 5ths.

> **CHECK YOUR UNDERSTANDING 15.1**
> Analyze the first three chords of this sequence with Roman numerals. Then, complete the sequence until it resolves to a tonic triad. Supply all Roman numerals.
>
>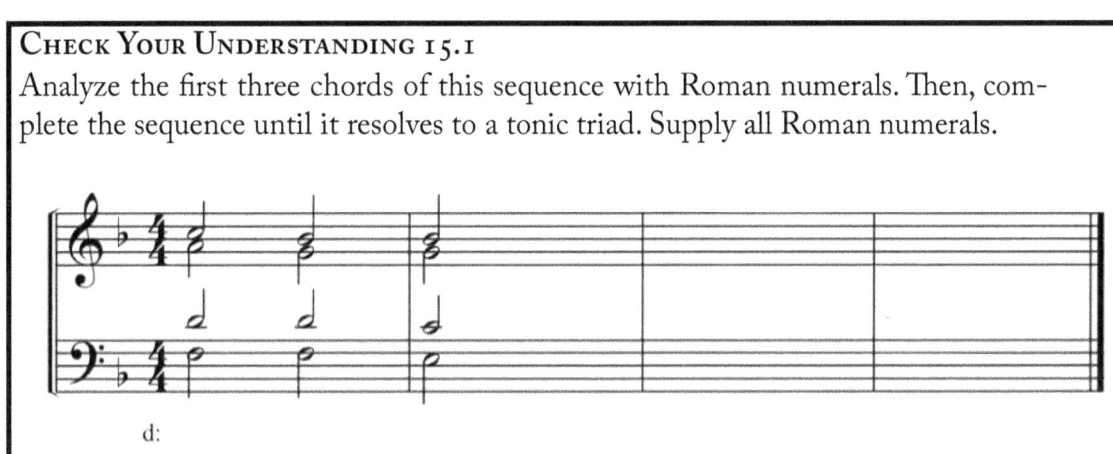
>
> d:

Exercise 15.1

Complete these sequences. End each progression by resolving to a triadic tonic chord. Use the examples in Chapter 15 as a guide.

Exercise 15.2

Complete this harmonization. Add additional non-chord tones as indicated.

Appendix A: Keys Around the Circle of Fifths

Keys and their corresponding key signatures are often presented in the form of a circle of 5ths. Such a presentation is a convenient way to organize the keys as well as a practical way to show how chords and key areas tend to move along or progress from one to another. Below is a diagram of the keys written as a **descending circle of 5ths**. While it may appear backwards from what is seen in other theory books, it is a more accurate picture of how chords usually progress in tonal music.

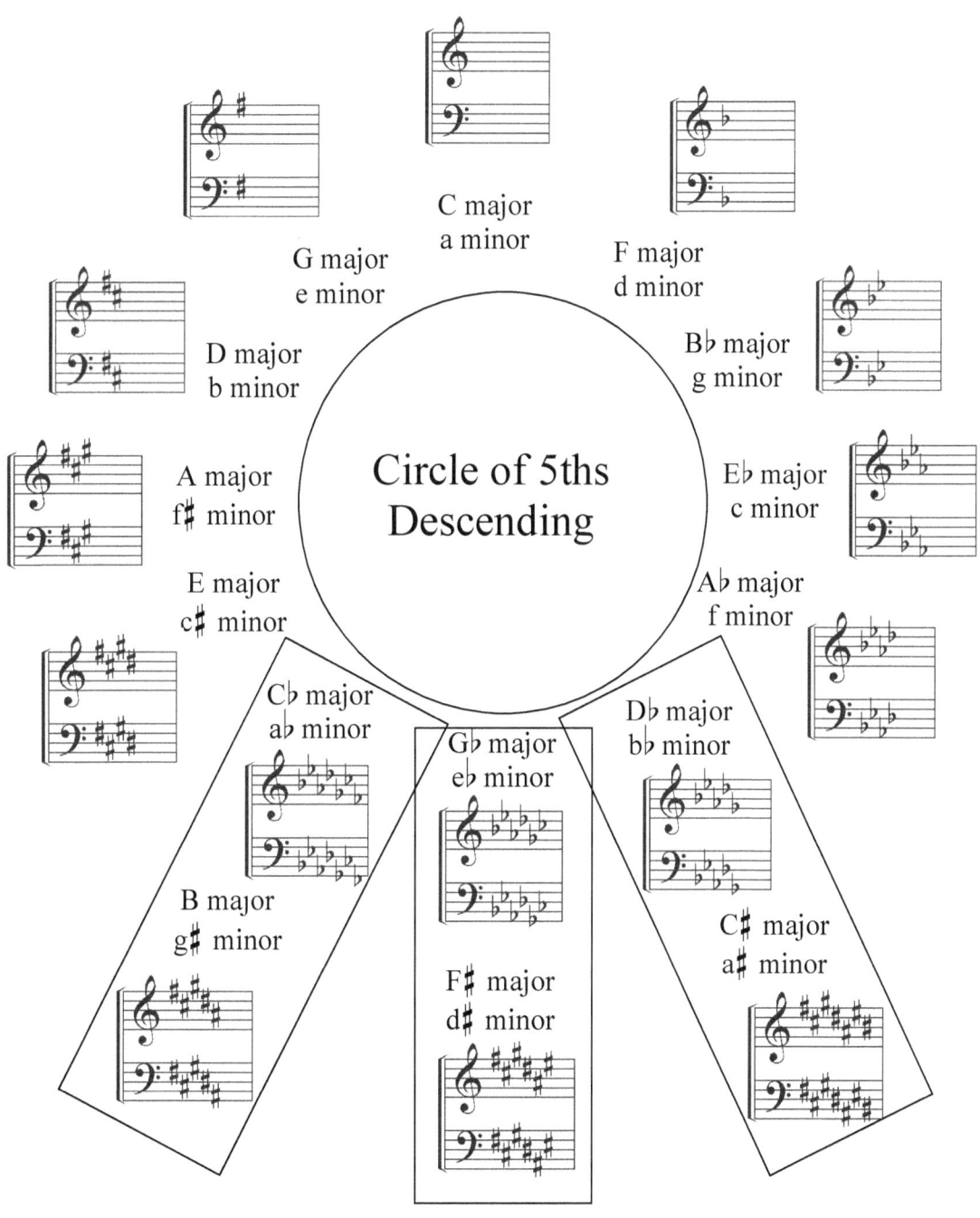

Appendix B: Qualities of Triads and Seventh Chords

Triads are three-note chords that are built using successive intervals of the third. For this reason, they are sometimes called **tertian harmony**. The quality of the thirds will determine the quality of the triad according to the chart below. The "half step formula" refers to the number of half steps from the root to the chord 3rd, and then from the chord 3rd to the chord 5th.

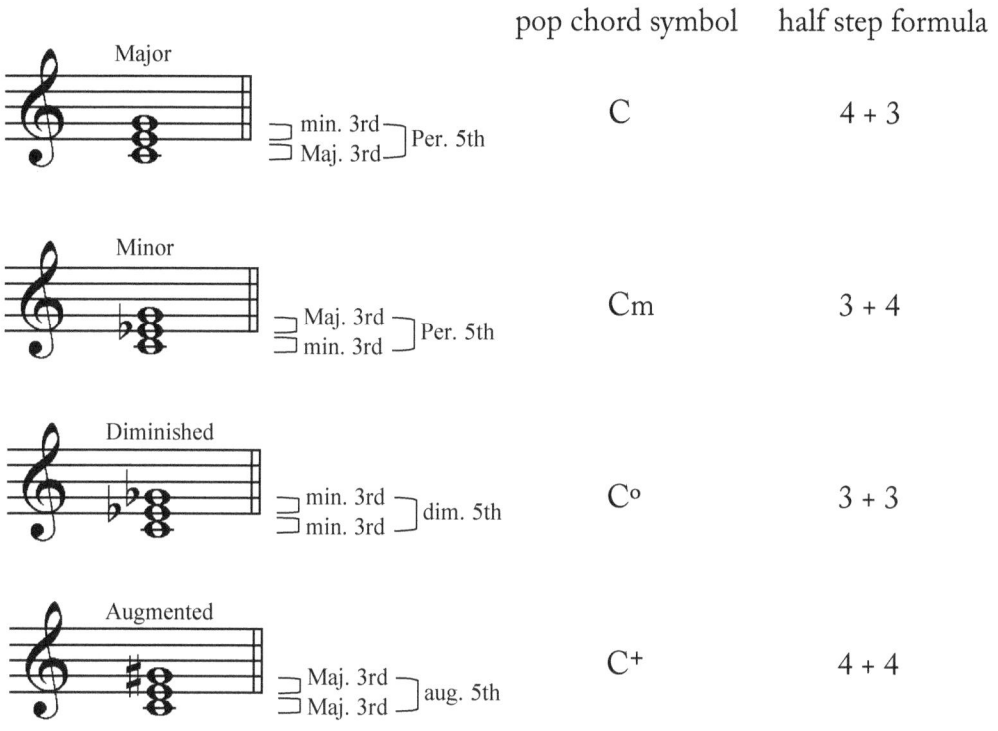

Seventh chords are triads with the addition of a seventh interval above the bass. We usually name their quality by identifying the quality of the triad followed by the quality of the 7th interval; hence, the label "major-major 7" (MM7) for the first seventh chord shown below.

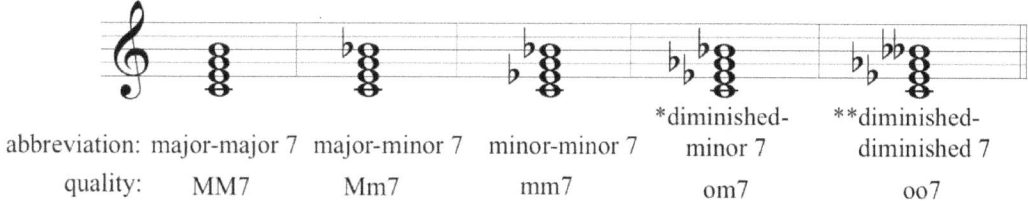

*The diminished–minor 7 chord is commonly called "half diminished." The symbol "ø7" is used to denote this chord quality in traditional Roman numeral analysis as well as with pop chord symbols.

**The diminished–diminished 7 chord is commonly called "fully diminished." The symbol "o7" is used to denote this chord quality in traditional Roman numeral analysis as well as with pop chord symbols.

Appendix C: Non Chord Tones 1

Terms and Concepts in This Chapter		
non chord tone	anticipation	neighbor group
passing tone	escape tone	incomplete neighbor tone
neighbor tone	appoggiatura	pedal point

A **non-chord tone** is a note that does not fit into the analysis of a chord. Composers allow themselves to write such notes, but usually under very controlled circumstances. A non-chord tone will always introduce dissonance, and the composer is concerned with how this dissonance is approached as well as how it is resolved.

Passing Tone (PT)

A passing tone:
- is a non-chord tone.
- occurs on a weak beat or weak part of a beat.
- is approached by step.
- is left by step in the same direction

Example C.1 - Passing Tones

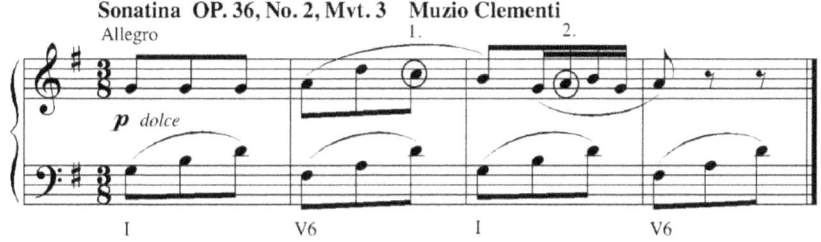

Do the circled notes fit all the criteria for a passing tone? Is there an alternate explanation for circled tone #1?

Neighbor Tone (NT)

A neighbor tone:
- is a non-chord tone.
- occurs on a weak beat or weak part of a beat.
- is approached by step.
- is left by step in the opposite direction (it returns to the tone that preceded it).

Example C.2 - Neighbor Tones

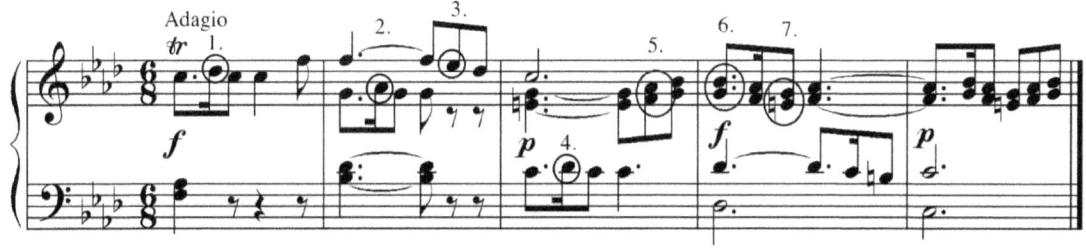

Do circled notes 1 and 2 fit all the criteria for a neighbor tone? Do you see any other neighbor tones among the circled tones? What is unusual about the circled pitches at number 5? Do the pitches at 6 and 7 resemble neighbor tones? If not, what are they?

Anticipation (ant.)

An anticipation:
- is a non-chord tone.
- occurs on a weak beat or weak part of a beat.
- is approached by step or leap.
- stays on the same pitch and is resolved as a result of the chord change. (It "anticipates" the chord tone.)

Example C.3 - Anticipations

The circled notes 1 and 2 are best explained as anticipations. Can you explanation notes 3 and 4?

Escape Tone (E.T.)

An escape tone:
- is a non-chord tone.
- occurs on a weak beat or weak part of a beat.
- is approached by step.
- is left by leap in the opposite direction.

Example C.4 - Escape Tone

Of all the circled non-chord tones, #6 fits the description of an escape tone. What are all the others?

Appoggiatura (app.)

An appoggiatura:
- is a non-chord tone.
- occurs on a strong beat or strong part of a beat.
- is often approached by leap.
- is left by step in the opposite direction.

Of the circled non-chord tones, #3 best fits the definition of an appoggiatura. What are the others?

Neighbor Group (Changing Tones) (N.G.)

Neighbor group characteristic:
- They are a pair of non-chord tones.
- They occurs on a relatively weaker metric position in the measure.
- The group is approached by step and left by step.
- The figure consists of a neighbor note below, followed by a neighbor note above the chord tone of resolution.
- The figure may also consist of a neighbor tone above followed by a neighbor tone below the chord tone of resolution

Mozart: Quartet in A Major, K. 464, mvt. 1

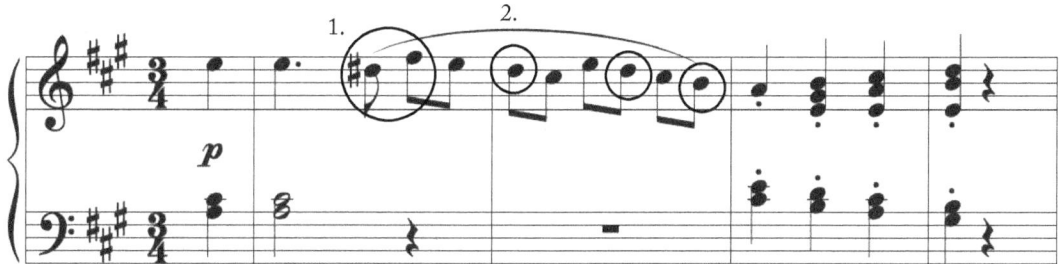

1. This is a neighbor group. D# is a neighbor below and F# is a neighbor above the chord tone E that occurs on the last eighth note of this measure.
2. These are passing tones. The first passing tone is called an **accented passing tone (A.P.T.)** because it occurs on the stronger part of the beat.

Incomplete Neighbor Tone (I.N.T)

An incomplete neighbor tone:
- is a non-chord tone.
- occurs on a weak beat or weak part of a beat. This is what distinguishes it from an appoggiatura.
- is approached by leap.
- is left by step in the opposite direction.

Bach, Prelude XX from the Well-Tempered Clavier, Book 1

Pedal Point (Pedal Tone) (Ped.)

A pedal point is a tone, often but not always in the bass voice, that extends through several harmonies. It can be analyzed as a chord tone when it fits with the harmony, or as a non-chord tone when it does not fit with the harmony.

Beethoven: Piano Sonata Op. 14, No. 1

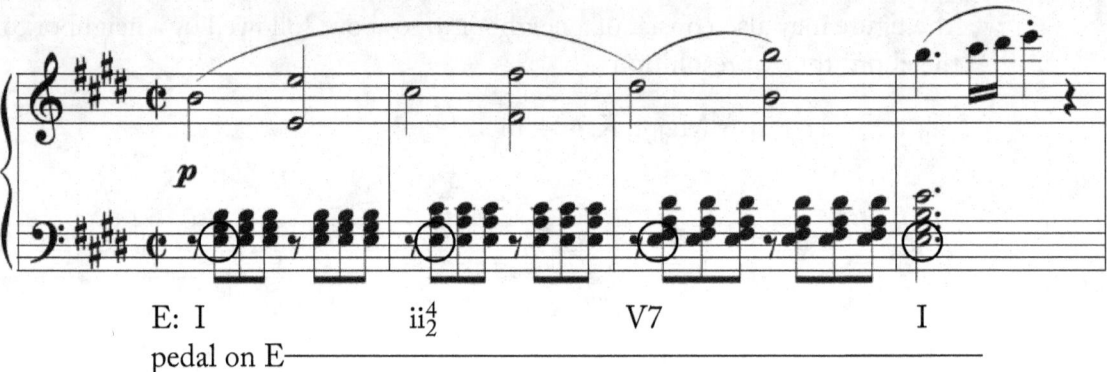

E: I　　　　　　　ii$_2^4$　　　　　V7　　　　　　I
pedal on E————————————————————————

You can see that the pitch E is in the lowest voice, and that it extends through the first four measures. In measures 1, 2, and 4, it can be analyzed as part of the chord structure of the upper voices. However, in the measure 3, it is a non-chord tone. When analyzing this measure, it is sufficient to analyze only the upper voices without regard to the pedal. The inversion does not need to be indicated because it is irrelevant when there is a pedal in the lowest voice. The analysis should show some indication that there is a pedal point, as shown above.

APPLICATION OF NON-CHORD TONES

Below is a two-measure phrase that has been repeated five times. Each time, an additional non-chord tone has been added with an explanation of its usage.

P.T. The passing tone fills the melodic space of a third.

N.T. The neighbor tone serves as an ornament to a tone that is stationary from chord to chord.

Ant. The anticipation introduces, in one voice, a chord tone of the following harmony in advance of the arrival of that harmony in the other voices.

E.T. The escape tone interrupts the motion of a descending, stepwise line.

App. The appoggiatura is an accented dissonance that is approached by leap and left by step in the opposite direction.

Exercise C1

Rewrite this two-measure phrase immediately to the right. Add at least one of each: P.T., N.T., Ant., E.T., App.

Appendix D: Non Chord Tones 2, The Suspension

TERMS AND CONCEPTS IN THIS CHAPTER		
preparation	suspension	resolution

Suspensions occur when the music progresses to the notes of a new harmony in all the voices except for one. This one voice becomes out of synchronization with the harmonic motion because it resolves into the new chord later in time than all the other voices. At the moment when the music is still retaining the pitch of the previous chord in one of the voices (in other words, suspending it), we call this a suspension. There are three elements of a suspension that will all occur in the same voice:

- The **Preparation (P)**. This is the pitch that is about to be suspended. There is nothing special about a preparation. It is simply one of the chord tones of the harmony when it first occurs.

- The **Suspension (S)**. This is when the progression changes to a new chord in all the voices except for one. This one voice is the same pitch and in the same voice as the preparation that was identified in the previous harmony. However, it is now a non-chord tone.

- The **Resolution (R)**. This is when the suspension moves stepwise down so that it joins the harmony as a chord tone.

EXAMPLE D.1 - THE 4 - 3 SUSPENSION

Notice that the pitch F, the preparation, is simply a note of the IV chord. However, when the progression moves on to the I chord, the pitch F has not moved and must be labeled as a suspension. Only on the following beat does the I chord come clearly into focus as the suspension becomes a resolution by moving stepwise down. In the vast majority of cases, the resolution is stepwise down. In the instances where the resolution resolves stepwise up, we call the figure a **retardation** rather than a suspension.

In example D.1, the **preparation is tied to the suspension.** This is extremely common, but not always necessary. However, it is necessary that **the preparation and the suspension are the same pitch and in the same voice**. Also, notice the figured bass designation of 4 – 3. We always reference the suspension and the resolution separated by a hyphen in the figured bass when labeling a suspension. These numbers, as in all figured bass numbers, refer to the intervals created above the bass.

Example D.2 below illustrates how to add a suspension to an existing progression:

Example D.2 - Creating Suspensions

Example a. above is written without any suspensions. Because there is stepwise descending motion in both the soprano and the tenor, there are excellent opportunities for the addition of suspensions.

In example b., the tenor pitch C in the I chord is tied over to the tenor pitch C in the V chord creating a suspension. Notice that the rhythm has to be adjusted to allow room for the suspension and the resolution that takes place on the following beat when the tenor moves stepwise down to B.

In example c., the soprano pitch E in the I chord is tied over to the soprano pitch E in the V chord creating a suspension. Notice that the rhythm has to be adjusted to allow room for the suspension and the resolution that takes place on the following beat when the soprano moves stepwise down to D.

You should circle and label the preparation, suspension, and resolution in examples b. and c. above.

Here are some rules to follow when creating a suspension.

- Suspensions happen in a voice that is resolving stepwise down. The effect of the suspension is to delay the resolution of one voice in a progression.
- You should always be able to identify three elements of this type of motion: the preparation, the suspension, and the resolution.
- The preparation, suspension, and resolution must all be in the same voice.
- Suspensions are approached by a preparation on the same pitch and are left by a resolution moving stepwise down.
- Suspensions should occur on a beat or part of a beat that is stronger than the resolution.

Suspensions can happen in any voice and can create a wide variety of intervals. Below is one additional example in which three suspensions have been created from stepwise motion.

Example D.3 - Creating Suspensions

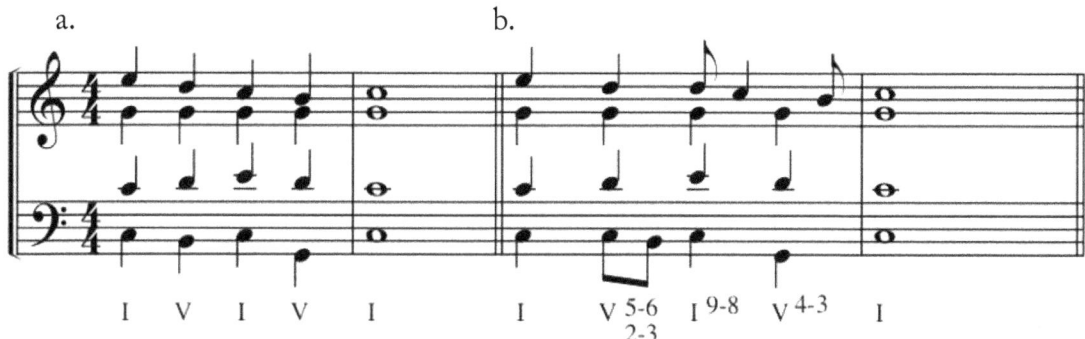

In example a., there are no suspensions, but the descending stepwise voice leading in the soprano and bass provides fertile ground for the creation of suspensions.

In example b., the V chord on beat 2 has a suspension in the bass. Although the preparation, suspension, and resolution are readily apparent, the resultant figured bass seems somewhat confusing. This is because the bass is moving and we are counting the intervals from the moving bass notes to stationary notes in the tenor and alto.

On beat 3 of example b., there is a 9-8 suspension in the soprano. This is the only type of suspension where the resolution tone (C) actually sounds in the bass at the same time as the suspension (D in the soprano). In all other suspensions, it is incorrect to include the resolution tone at the same time as the suspension in another voice.

On beat 4 of example b., there is another suspension in the soprano. In this case, the resolution of the previous 9-8 suspension (on the second half of beat 3 in the soprano) is also the preparation for the 4-3 suspension on beat 4. This type of succession of suspensions is called a **chain of suspensions**.

You should identify all the suspensions in example B.3 (b.) by circling and labeling with P, S, and R.

Exercise D.1

Rewrite each example to produce the suspensions indicated.

Appendix E: Figured Bass Harmonization

Figured bass symbols are written below the bass line and refer to intervals that must be written above the bass to create chords and non-chord tones. The numbers refer to a certain pitch, or to a combination of pitches, but the exact voice or octave location is not indicated. Thus, the rules of voice leading must be clearly understood to produce a satisfying result. Figured bass is often written in a kind of shorthand, so not all intervals above the bass will be indicated. In fact, 5ths and 3rds are often not indicated.

This type of figured bass notation was commonly used in basso continuo parts in the 17th and 18th centuries. In those practices, an accompaniment would be improvised on a chording instrument such as a lute, organ, or harpsichord. The continuo player would read the bass part and use the figured bass numbers to create the harmony above while accompanying an instrumental or vocal ensemble.

Below is a summary of procedures to follow when realizing a figured bass:

- For each bass pitch, supply a harmonization in four parts using good voice leading.

- Use root position chords unless the inversion symbol indicates otherwise. In other words, if there is nothing written below the bass pitch, assume that the bass is the root of the chord and write a root position triad.

- If 6 is written below the bass pitch, assume that the bass is the third of the chord and write a first inversion triad.

- If $^6_4$ is written below the bass pitch, assume that the bass is the fifth of the chord and write a second inversion triad.

- Be careful when writing the melody. It should have a satisfying shape and it should not create any voice leading problems with the bass.

- Chromatic alterations of pitches are indicated with accidentals in the figured bass or with a diagonal slash through a number. If an accidental is placed immediately to the left of a figured bass number, simply apply that accidental to the pitch that represents that interval above the bass.

- If an accidental appears in the figured bass without an accompanying number, assume that it is to be applied to the pitch that is a third above the bass.

- If there is a slash through a number, as in $\cancel{6}$, you should raise the pitch represented by that number by one half step using whatever accidental is appropriate.

Examine the figured bass below and read the explanation for each symbol:

Example E.1 - Figured Bass

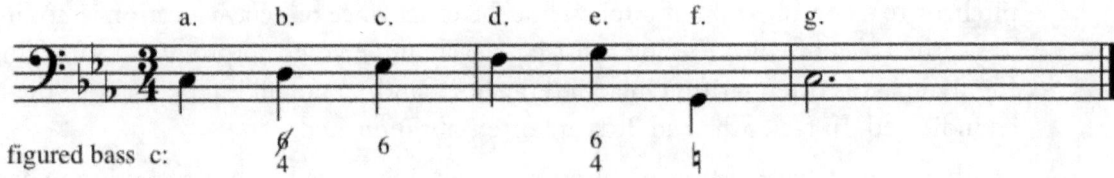

a. Nothing is indicated in the figured bass, so we will write a root position triad above the bass.

b. The $^6_4$ indicates that the D in the bass must be the 5th of the chord, and we should write a triad in second inversion. The slash through the 6 indicates that the sixth note above the bass should be raised from B♭ to B♮.

c. The 6 indicates that the bass pitch is the 3rd of the chord, and we should write a triad in first inversion.

d. Nothing is indicated in the figured bass, so we will write a root position triad above the bass.

e. The $^6_4$ indicates that the G in the bass must be the 5th of the chord, and we should write a triad in second inversion.

f. The ♮ in the figured bass is a shorthand way of indicating an alteration to the pitch that is a 3rd above the bass. We will change the 3rd above the bass from B♭ to B♮. Since there are no other numbers that indicate otherwise, we will write a triad in root position.

g. Nothing is indicated in the figured bass, so we will write a root position triad above the bass.

Below is a harmonization of the figured bass with good voice leading:

Example E.1 - Realized Figured Bass

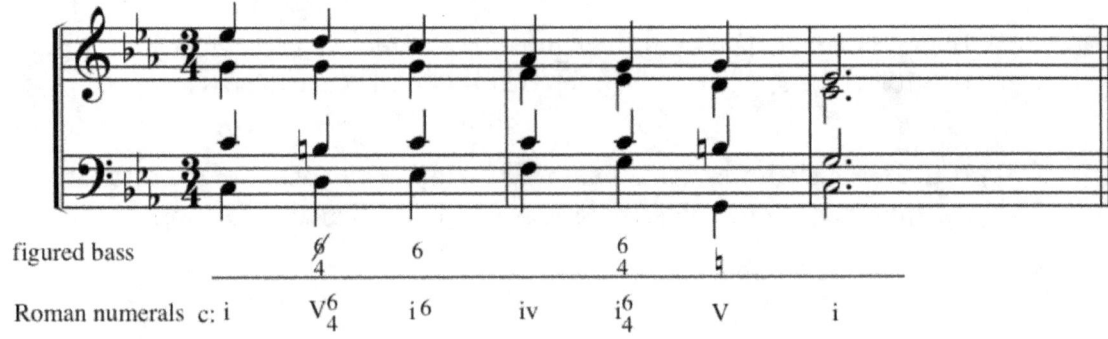

Appendix F: Piano Harmonization Exercises

Appendix G: Repertoire for Analysis

Bach, Johann Sebastian: Menuet from the French Suite in D minor   140
Beethoven, Ludwig van: Sonate Opus 49 No. 2 – Part 1   141
Beethoven, Ludwig van: Sonate Opus 49 No. 2 – Part 2   142
Bergmüller, J. F. T.: L'Arabesque   143
Fabe, Waltom, Hemy: Faith of Our Fathers   144
Handel, Georg Fredrich: Menuet I, from the Aylesford Pieces   145
Handel, Georg Fredrich: Menuet , from the Aylesford Pieces   146
Handel, Georg Fredrich: Air, from the Aylesford Pieces   147
Mozart, Wolfgang Amadeus: Sonata Opus KV 331, Mvt 1, Tema   148
Mozart, Wolfgang Amadeus: Sonata Opus KV 331, Rondo Alla Turca   149
Mozart, Wolfgang Amadeus: Sonata K457, Allegro assai   150
Schumann, Robert: Album for the Young, No. 2   151
Schumann, Robert: Album for the Young, No. 4   152
Schumann, Robert: Album for the Young, No. 8   153
Schumann, Robert: Album for the Young, No. 9   154
Schumann, Robert: Album for the Young, No. 14   155
Schumann, Robert: Album for the Young, No. 16   156
Schumann, Robert: Album for the Young, No. 18   157
Schumann, Robert: Traümerei, from Kinderscenen   158
Wesley, Charles: Hymn of Eve   159

THEORETIC CONCEPTS INDEX:

Anticipation   142, 146
Appoggiatura   141, 148, 149
Authentic sequence   140
Cadential $\substack{6\\4}$ 142, 143, 145, 148, 149, 150, 152, 156, 158
Deceptive resolution of V   144, 154,
First inversion triads   140, 141, 142, 143, 144, 145, 146, 147, 148, 149, 150, 152, 153, 154, 155, 156, 157, 158, 159
Escape tone   143, 145, 146, 147, 157
Neighbor tone   140, 142, 143, 144, 146, 147, 148, 149, 156, 157
Primary and secondary triads   140, 141, 142, 143, 144, 145, 146, 147, 148, 149, 150, 151, 152, 153, 154, 155, 156, 157, 158
Passing tone   140, 141, 142, 143, 145, 146, 147, 148, 149, 150, 152, 156, 157, 158
Passing $\substack{6\\4}$ 146, 148, 152
Pedal $\substack{6\\4}$ 141, 142, 143, 144, 148, 153, 156,
Pedal tone   141, 143, 148, 153, 155, 156, 157*, 158
Phrygian cadence   154,
Retardation   158
Seventh chords   140, 141, 143, 144, 145, 146, 148, 150, 151, 152, 154, 156, 157, 158
Seventh chords in inversion   141, 142, 146, 148, 150, 151, 152, 154, 156, 157, 158
Suspension   140, 144, 150, 158

Menuet
from French Suite in D Minor

J. S. Bach
1685 – 1750

Piano Sonata, Op. 49, No. 2

Part 1

Ludwig van Beethoven
1770 – 1827

Piano Sonata, Op. 49, No. 2

Part 2

Ludwig van Beethoven
1770 – 1827

Tempo di Menuetto

L'Arabesque

Johann Friedrich Tranz Bergmüller
1806 - 1874

Faith of Our Fathers

text: F. W. Faber, J. G. Walton
Music: H. F. Hemy
Setting: J. G. Walton

Menuet I
fron the Aylesford Pieces

Georg Frideric Handel
1685 - 1759

Menuet
fron the Aylesford Pieces

Georg Frideric Handel
1685 - 1759

Air
fron the Aylesford Pieces

Georg Frideric Handel
1685 - 1759

Movement 1: Tema
from Piano Sonata No 11

Wolfgang Amadeus Mozart
1756 – 1791

Rondo Alla Turca
from Piano Sonata No 11

Wolfgang Amadeus Mozart
1756 – 1791

Sonata K457

Wolfgang Amadeus Mozart
1756 – 1791

Soldiers' March
from *Album for the Young*

Robert Schumann
1810 – 1856

Chorale
from *Album for the Young*

Robert Schumann
1810 – 1856

Freue dich, o meine Seele.

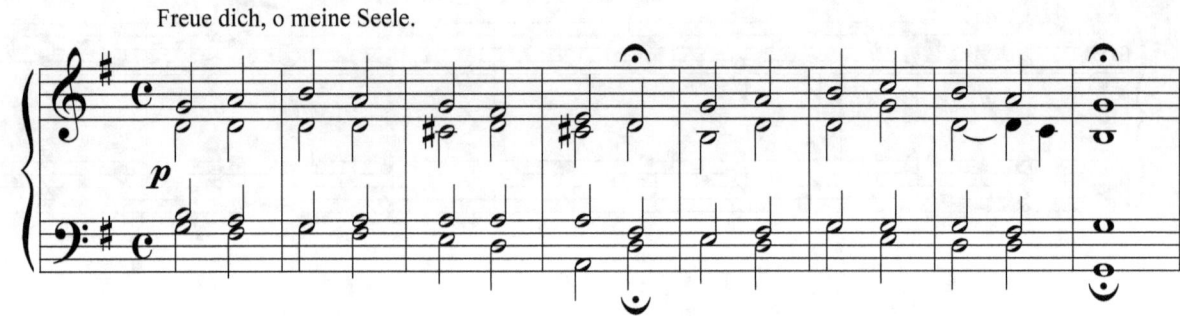
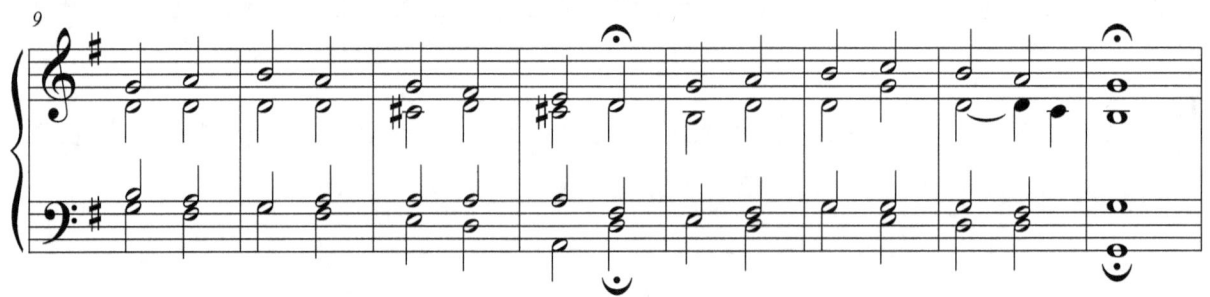

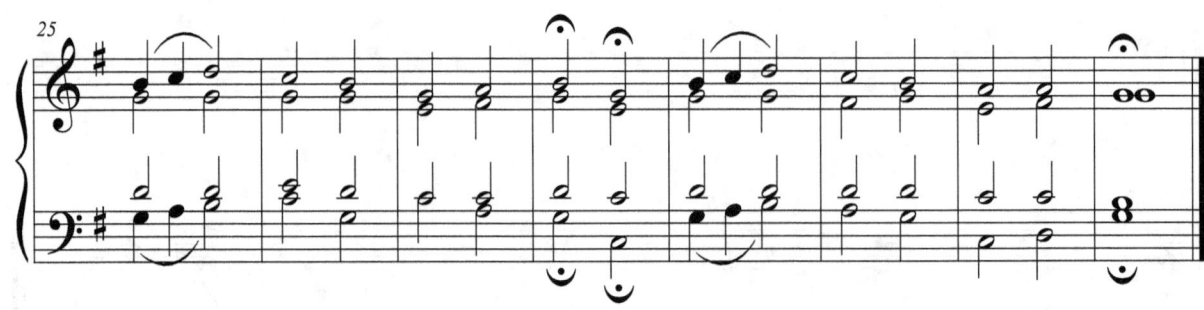

The Wild Rider
from *Album for the Young*

Robert Schumann
1810 – 1856

Folk Song

from *Album for the Young*

Robert Schumann
1810 – 1856

Little Etude
from *Album for the Young*

Robert Schumann
1810 – 1856

Leise und sehr egal zu spielen
(lightly and very evenly)

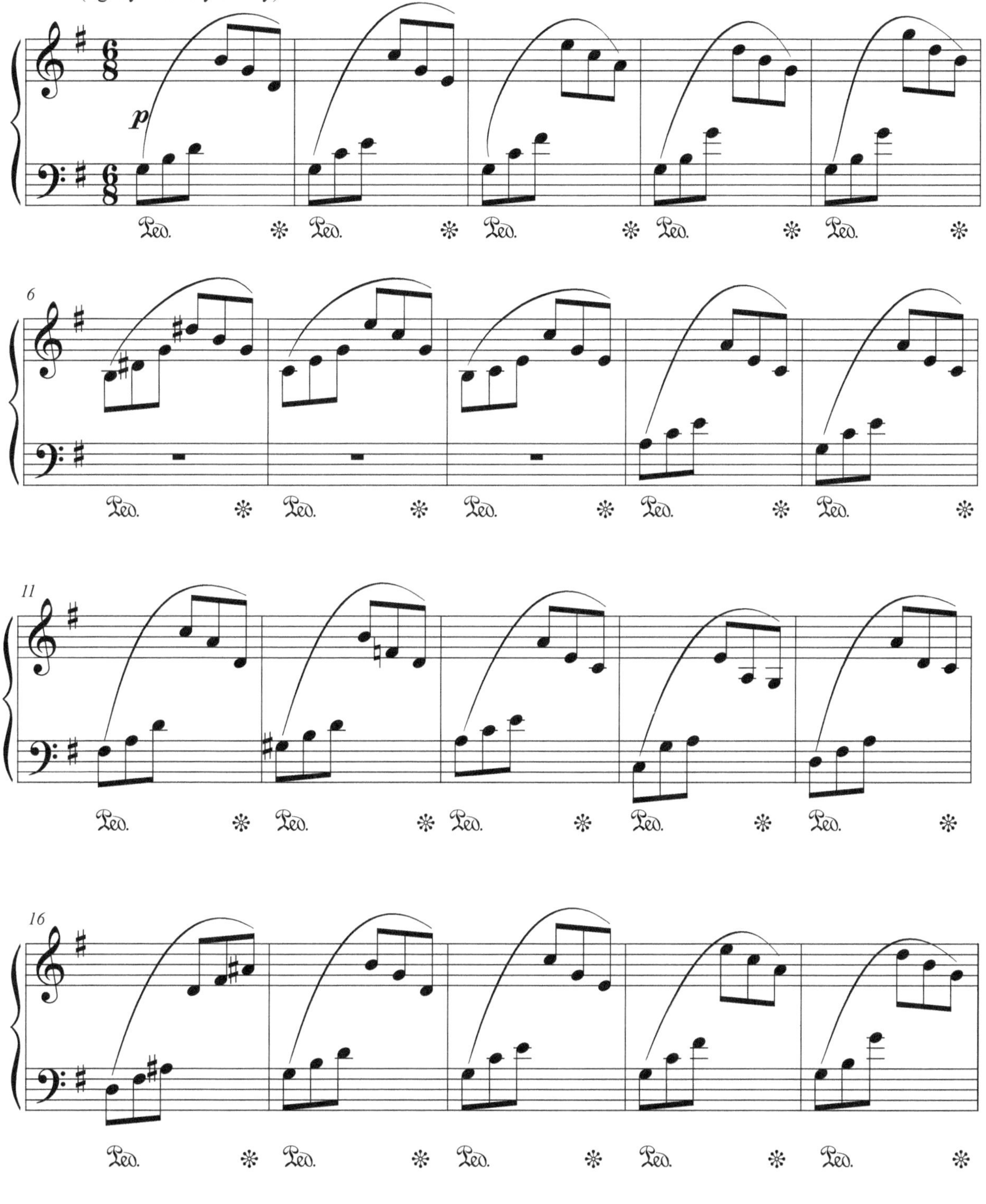

Erster Verlust
First Loss

Robert Schumann (1810 - 1856)
Album für die Jugend (Album for the Young)

The Reaper's Song
from *Album for the Young*

Robert Schumann
1810 – 1856

Traümerei
from *Kinderscenen*

Hymn of Eve

Charles Wesley

Appendix H: Harmonization Project

Pick one of the following well-known melodies to harmonize. Set the melody four different ways:

- Four-part chorale style
- Piano voicing
- Activated piano voicing
- One additional activated style of your choosing

Follow the examples given on the next page.

Example:

Step 1. Choose harmonies.

Step 2. Harmonize in four parts while improving the harmonization with inversions and sevenths.

Step 3. Set in piano voicing.

Step 4. Set in activated piano voicing.

Step 5 (optional). Create one more activated piano style of your choosing.

Appendix I: Check Your Understanding Answers

1.1

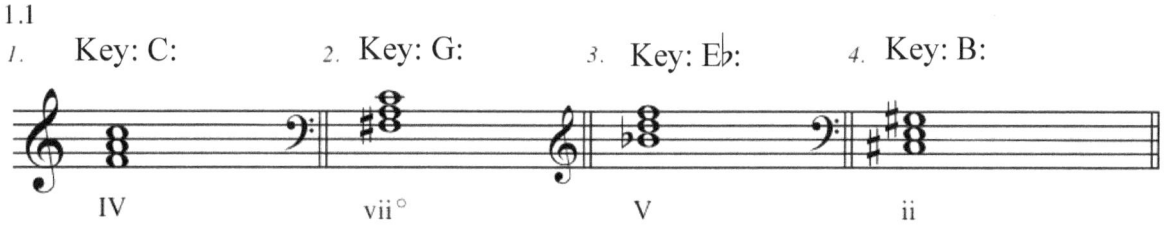

2.1

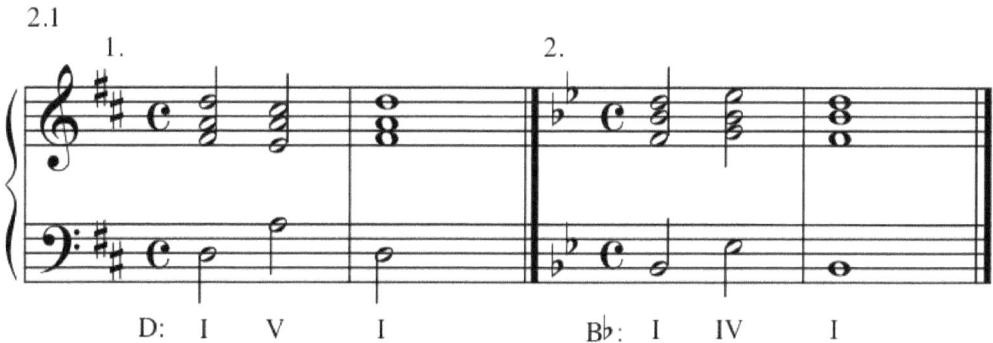

3.1

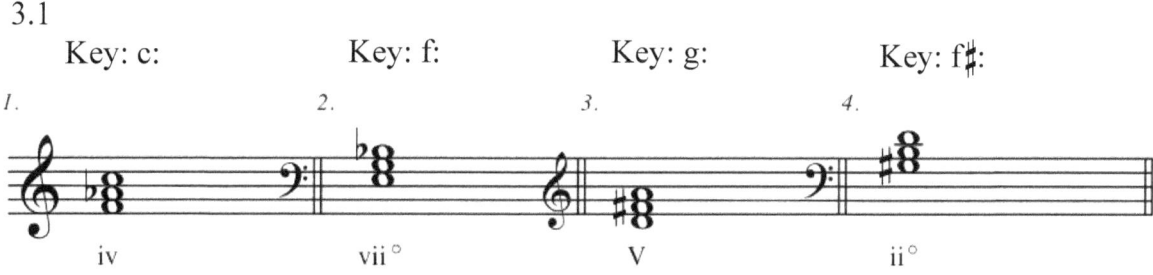

4.1

4.2

5.1

5.2

1. Soprano and alto out of their range. Harmonic distance too large between the alto and tenor.
2. Melodic distance in the tenor too large.
3. Incorrect doubling.
4. Harmonic distance between the tenor and alto too large.
5. Incorrect doubling.
6. Harmonic distance between the tenor and alto too large.
7. Crossed voices. Incorrect doubling.

6.1

6.2

7.1

7.2

8.1

8.2

9.1

9.2

9.3

9.4

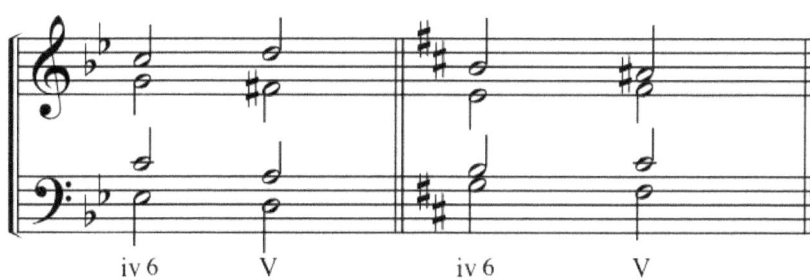

10.1

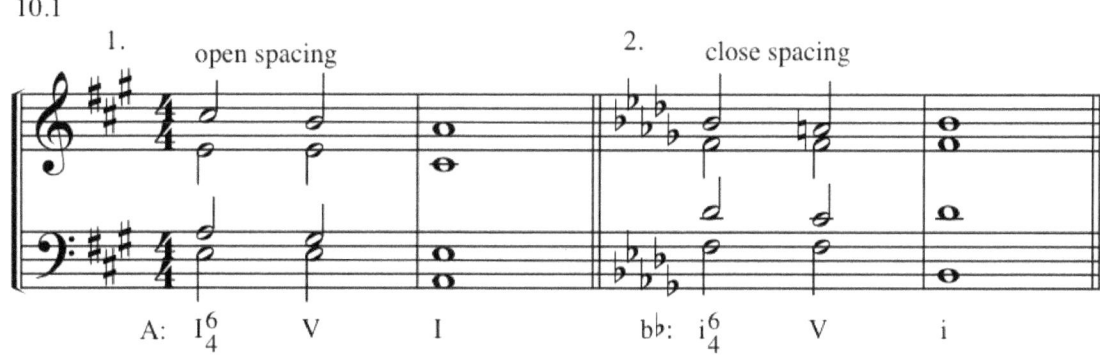

11.1

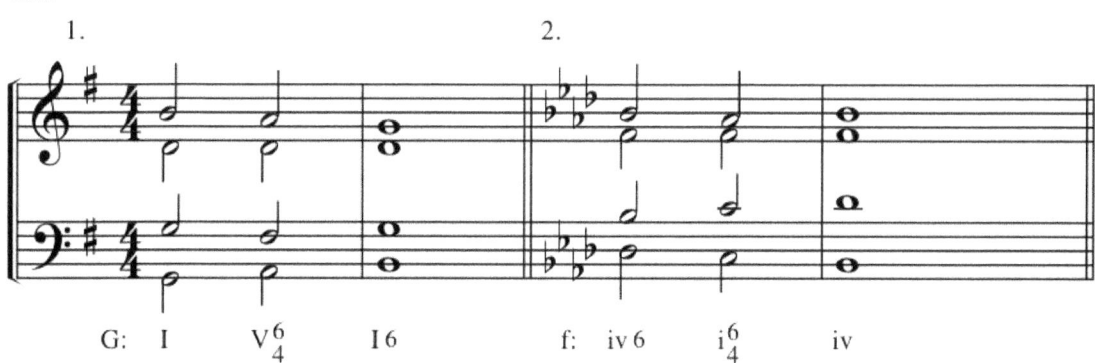

11.2
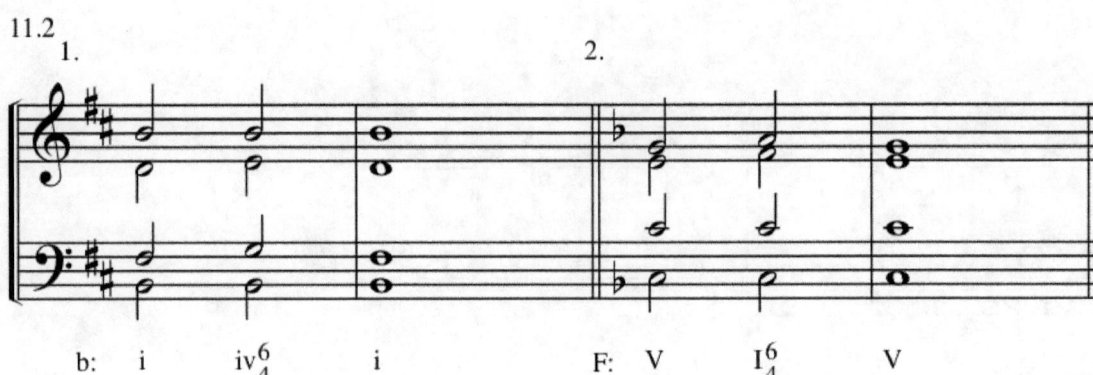

12.1

12.2

12.3

Index

A

activated piano voicing 159
anticipation 121
appoggiatura 122
authentic cadence 35, 36, 37, 44, 51
authentic sequence 113-115

C

cadences 36
    authentic cadence 36
    deceptive cadence 59, 61
        in minor key
            irregular doubling 61
    half cadence 35, 36, 37, 44, 51, 71
    imperfect 37
    perfect 37
    Phrygian half cadence 71-72
    plagal cadence 37, 44, 51
cadential $^6_4$ 78
    doubling and usage of 78
    rhythmic placement of 79
    usage and tonal function of 78
circle of 5ths
    descending 117
close spacing 8, 9, 11, 19-23, 28
crossed voices 28, 29, 34, 68

D

deceptive cadence 59, 61
    in minor key 60
diatonic triads
    in harmonic minor 13, 13–18, 13–18
    in major key 1–6
    in melodic minor 14–18
diminished triad 2, 14, 67, 70, 71, 106
direct 5ths and 8ves 30
dominant 1–6, 2, 7, 35, 36, 52, 57, 59, 68, 71, 78, 84, 85, 91, 106, 107
Dominant 1, 58
dominant 7th chord
    inversions of 101-102
        figured bass symbols for 101
        voice leading for 101-102
    leading tone resolving downward 93
    omitted 5th in 92
    structure of 91
    tendency tones in 91
    tritone in 91
    voice leading of 92, 94
        avoiding problems with 93
doubling
    for root position triads 23
    for first inversion triads 67, 69
    for first inversion diminished triads 70
    for second inversion triads 77

E

escape tone 122

F

figured bass 133

H

half cadence 35, 36, 37, 44, 51, 71
harmonic function 35
    dominant 35, 57
    dominant preparation 35, 57
    tonic 35, 57
harmonic interval
    limitations in adjacent voices 28
harmonic minor scale 13-18
harmonic rhythm 52
harmonize 7
    harmonizing a melody 51
        mistakes with 51
    in four parts 20–26
    piano voicing 7–12, 8, 9, 19, 20, 21, 23, 159, 160

I

incomplete neighbor tone 122
inversions (of triads) 67-72
    first inversion
        diminished triad usage and doubling 70
        doubling rule for 67, 69
        figured bass label for 67
        usages of 68
    second inversion 77
        arpeggiating $^6_4$ 77
        cadential $^6_4$ 78
        doubling rule for 77
        figured bass designation of 77
        passing $^6_4$
        pedal $^6_4$
        tonal functions of 77

L

leading tone 1, 2, 35, 42, 91-94, 101, 102, 106-108, 115
    raised leading tone 13, 42
    resolution of 60, 92, 93, 94, 101, 102, 106, 107

M

major triad 2, 14, 40, 67, 69
mediant 1-6
melodic intervals
    forbidden melodic intervals
        augmented 2nd 42
        tritone 42
melodic leap
    limitations in inner voices 28
melodic minor scale 14–18
minor scale
    seventh chords in 106
    triads in the harmonic minor scale 13
    triads in the melodic minor scale 14
    minor triad 2, 14, 67, 69
motion
    contrary 27
    no motion 27
    oblique 27
    parallel 27, see also *parallel motion*
    similar 27

N

neighbor group 122
neighbor tone 121
non chord tone
    application of 122
    appoggiatura 122
    escape tone 122
    incomplete neighbor tone 122
    neighbor group 122
    neighbor tone 121
    passing tone 121
    suspension 127
non-chord tone 121
    anticipation 121

O

open spacing 21–26
    process for creating 21–26
overlapped voices 52, 68, 69
    definition of 68
overtone series 30
    as it related to dominant 35
    fundamental 30

P

parallel motion 27–34
    conecutive 5ths by contrary motion 30
    parallel 5ths 30
        finding 52
    parallel 8ves 30
    parallel unisons 30
    process for finding forbidden parallels 30
    unequal 5ths 30
passing $^6_4$
    usage and functions of 83
passing tone 121
pedal point 122
pedal $^6_4$
    usage and functions of 84
phrase 35
    antecedent-consequent 37
Phrygian half cadence 71-72
piano harmonization 135
piano voicing 7–12, 8, 9, 19, 20, 21, 23, 159, 160
plagal cadence 37, 44, 51
pop chord symbol 2–6
primary triads 57
progression 58
    progression paths 58

R

retardation 127
retrogression 52
Roman numeral 2, 2–6, 8, 14, 19, 119
root position 8–12
root tone motion 37
    progression in 2nds
        voice leading procedure for 41
    progression in 3rds
        voice leading procedure 58
    progression in 5ths
        alaternate procedure 53
        voice leading procedure for 39

S

scale degrees 1
secondary triads 57
    functions of 57
sequence 113
    authentic sequence 113-115
        in a major key 113
        in a minor key 114
seventh chords 91
    diatonic 7th chords in a major key 91, 105
    diatonic 7th chords in a minor key 106
    dominant 7th chord 91

     leading tone 7th chords 107
     qualities of 119
         fully diminished 105, 108
         half diminished 105, 107
         major-major 7 105
         major-minor 7 105
         minor-minor 7 105
     supertonic 7th chords 106
similar motion 27, 28
subdominant 2
submediant 2
supertonic 1
suspension 127-129
     chain of 129
     creation of 128
     preparation 127
     resolution 127

T

tertian harmony 119
tonic 1, 2, 7, 13, 35-38
triads
     diminished triad 2, 14, 67, 70, 71, 106
     major triad 2, 14, 40, 67, 69
     minor triad 2, 14, 67, 69
     qualities of 119

V

voice leading
     errors in 34
     good characteristics of 28
voice ranges
     alto 19
     bass 19
     soprano 19–26
     tenor 19–26

www.ingramcontent.com/pod-product-compliance
Lightning Source LLC
LaVergne TN
LVHW081550060526
838201LV00054B/1841